Growtl
the Mo

EDITED BY SOO DARCY

Head of events and books
Leah Darbyshire

Editor
Laura Slater

Published by ARK Group:

UK, Europe and Asia office
6–14 Underwood Street
London, N1 7JQ
United Kingdom
Tel: +44(0) 207 566 5792
publishing@ark-group.com

North America office
4408 N. Rockwood Drive, Suite 150
Peoria IL 61614
United States
Tel: +1 (309) 495 2853
publishingna@ark-group.com

www.ark-group.com

Printed by Canon (UK) Ltd, Cockshot Hill, Reigate, RH2 8BF, United Kingdom

ISBN: 978-1-78358-244-0

A catalogue record for this book is available from the British Library

ARK Group is a division of Wilmington plc. The company is registered in England & Wales with company number 2931372 GB. Registered office: 6–14 Underwood Street, London N1 7JQ. VAT Number: GB 899 3725 51.

Contents

Part 2: **Case Studies**

Executive summary

It is logical that any business that is not growing at least in line with market conditions and the competition cannot hope to survive, let alone thrive. Since the recession of 2008/2009, law firms that once saw growth as easy and inevitable are finding that the only way to achieve this is now to wrest market share from the competition. There is no one "right" way to do this; some firms have opted for a determined policy of buying market share and recruiting lateral talent, while others rely on more organic growth. With contributions from a wide range of thought leaders and consultants, this book provides advice on the growth options available, and shares practical guidance designed to help firm leaders to formulate and implement a profitable, sustainable growth strategy.

The book is divided into two sections: the first provides practical insight and guidance; and the second comprises case studies from a range of law firms from the US and UK who share their own secrets to successful, durable growth.

As the first contributor, Andrew Hedley of Hedley Consulting, points out: "If you're not growing you're going backwards." Firms need to grow not just to cope with rising costs and downward pressure on price, but also to enable them to invest in staff, resources, and service delivery. The opening chapter in this book discusses the imperative to grow and various strategies to do so, including advice on market positioning, client retention, pricing strategy, and culture and performance management.

How much do your top clients contribute to the success of your firm? When it comes to your key assets they can be an invaluable source of growth, and conversely their loss can be devastating to the bottom line. In Chapter 2, Robert Pay, business development director at Alvarez & Marsal, describes how a key relationship management program can help firms to consistently retain and grow those clients and referral sources that are the most important to the health of your business. This chapter includes a questionnaire to test your readiness and suitability for a key relationship program, advice on how to overcome typical barriers you may encounter, and a how-to guide to assembling the teams necessary to design and manage your key relationship plan.

When it comes to determining a strategic direction to take, many firm leaders find themselves with too many options, and too many interested parties. When so many voices and opinions must be taken into account, who should you listen to? The answer, according to Susan Pettit, founder and managing director of Client Central, is *your clients*. After all, who knows better than the client just how they would define "value", or what they are looking for beyond practical legal advice? This chapter describes how to implement a client listening program to better serve clients, enable stronger relationships, and create a platform for differentiation and growth.

The arguments for promoting a culture of cross-selling within a firm are obvious, but equally obvious are the challenges of selling those arguments to a wider partnership who may be deeply protective (or even possessive) of relationships that have been carefully nurtured over the years. Expert advice is provided from renowned business development coach David H. Freeman, who describes in the next chapter how to drive cross-selling from the top and make it a cornerstone of your growth strategy and of your firm's culture.

Many firms are adopting a proactive strategy of growth through lateral hires. But while bringing in a fee earner with an existing book of business may seem like a quick win, a startling number of lateral moves fail to see the expected benefits. In the next chapter, the chief marketing officer at Freeborn & Peters LLP, Ian Turvill, describes the critical success factors that can help your firm to get it right.

While law firms strive to extract more work from their clients, general counsel are under greater pressure to keep more work in house and to prove their value through visible revenue growth. In the final chapter, Deepa Tharmaraj, legal director at Dell, provides the in-house perspective on innovation and growth in a lean in-house legal department.

Part two of this book comprises case studies from firms who describe their own (proven) strategies for growing revenue and market share. In the first of these, the chief marketing and business development officer at Stinson Leonard Street, Jill Weber, describes how the firm's "Fast Forward" program provides attorneys with a systematic approach to business development, helping them to build larger and more durable practices.

Following on from this, in the second case study – from the UK's largest litigation-only firm, Stewarts Law – managing partner and co-founder John Cahill describes the firm's laser-like focus on complex, high-value matters which serves as a key differentiator, and has led to considerable organic growth and outstanding PEP.

In the final case study, from Levenfeld Pearlstein LLC, executive director Angela Hickey describes how the firm's holistic approach to improving client experience drives client retention, employee satisfaction, and growth.

About the authors

John Cahill is the managing partner of Stewarts Law LLP and chairman of the executive committee and risk management committee. He took over the role of managing partner in 2000, 10 years after he co-founded the firm. His objective in 2000 was to refocus the firm and thereby create a firm specializing in high-value complex disputes only. Today, Stewarts Law is a Top 100 firm and the largest litigation-only firm in the UK.

John is frequently described as the "architect" of the current Stewarts Law business model. His experience (over 25 years) of dealing with a wide range of complex civil disputes has informed the firm's choice of specialist litigation areas and supported the promotion and growth of the firm.

Although not now an active fee earner, John is a member of all departmental risk assessment committees, which decide whether or not to accept instruction on a case if it is to be funded on a contingent or conditional fee basis. Correct litigation risk assessment at the outset has been and will continue to be a key component of the firm's success. John is also keen to ensure that individual practice areas are supported by a system of clear and effective management. In 2010, Stewarts Law was delighted to see this "fundamental" acknowledged when it was voted Best Managed Professional Firm at Managing Partners' Forum's European Practice Management Awards.

In the last 10 years, John has spearheaded the launch of the firm's divorce and family, aviation and travel, commercial litigation, employment, competition litigation, international arbitration, tax litigation, and trust litigation departments.

David H. Freeman, JD is a former practicing lawyer, the award-winning CEO of the David Freeman Consulting Group, and founder of Law Firm Culture*Shift*®. He is a best-selling author, speaker, consultant, and coach who has shown thousands of lawyers and professionals how to become more effective leaders and rainmakers.

For three consecutive years, David was recognized nationally as the top "Law Firm Business Development Consultant and Coach" in *National Law Journal* surveys, and for over 20 years he has worked with hundreds of law firms worldwide, including over one-third of the AmLaw 200. He is the author of four books: *The Law Firm Leader's Reference Guide for Creating a Business Development Culture*; *Secrets of the Masters: The Business Development Guide for Lawyers*; *Weekly Reminders for Revenue-Focused Leaders*; and *Creating a Cross-Serving CultureShift: Mastering Cross-selling for Lawyers and Leaders*.

David is a highly rated speaker, trainer, and consultant, and his expertise has been recognized through appointments as an elected fellow in the College of Law Practice Management, and as the exclusive business development coach for the Women in Law Empowerment Forum (WILEF). He also brings a deep understanding of how to engage the organizational and human factors that drive successful implementation based on several years as a change management, strategic planning, and balanced scorecard consultant for mid-sized and large corporations. He brings all of his expertise together in his proprietary Law Firm Culture*Shift*® process, a whole firm methodology that dramatically increases client and revenue-focused activity throughout a firm. He can be reached at 949–715–0819 or David@LawFirmCultureShift.com.

Andrew Hedley helps the leaders of law firms to create mold-breaking strategies, develop strong brands, forge robust client relationships, and design compelling propositions. In addition to his strategic project advice, Andrew is much sought after as a strategy group guide, partner retreat speaker, workshop facilitator, and moderator. He is a respected contributor to specialist strategy and management publications and a regular keynote conference speaker. He is the author of three other ARK Group publications: *The Law Firm Merger: A Leader's Guide to Strategy & Realisation* (2014), *Client Strategy in a Changing Legal Market* (2011), and *Developing Strategic Client Relationships* (2008).

Following his MA, Andrew completed an MBA in 1993. Both focused on professional services strategy and business development. He has approaching 25 years' experience of managing and advising professional services firms, with more than 15 years focused on the legal sector, prior to which he was the managing director of an architectural practice. He was the business development director of two leading international law firms for nine years before establishing Hedley Consulting in 2005.

Andrew is a member of the Advisory Panel of NetworkMP, a leading peer network for managing partners of professional services firms. He sits on the judging panel of the Managing Partners' Forum (MPF) European Practice Management Awards and The Lawyer Management Awards. He is the course director of the Cambridge Marketing College CIM Professional Diploma in Professional Services Marketing, the only CIM accredited qualification focused on the needs of the professional services sector.

Andrew has been admitted as a fellow of the Institute of Directors, the Strategic Planning Society, the Chartered Management Institute, Cambridge Marketing College, and the Royal Society of Art. He can be contacted at: andrew.hedley@hedleyconsulting.com. For more information, see: www.hedleyconsulting.com.

Angela Hickey is executive director of Levenfeld Pearlstein, overseeing LP's business operations with the philosophy that change can only be driven by trust built through transparency. Applying this philosophy to her own role within the firm, she has become one of LP's most trusted and influential leaders, paving the way for the development of many of the innovative business strategies that help to make the firm a marketplace leader. This includes orchestrating the successful execution of the LP Way through her position as a member of the firm's executive and compensation committees, and using her influence there to broaden perspectives and systems within the firm.

Robert Pay started his career in London, working in advertising as an account manager for a number of multinational clients. He first got involved in key relationship management at Deloitte Haskins & Sells, where he worked as marketing manager for the banking and securities practice both for the UK and the international firm. He was then recruited by Clifford Chance to establish its first marketing function and set up a key relationship program, the first in a major law firm.

Robert served at the London Stock Exchange as head of marketing where he partnered with investment banks to develop a successful campaign to compete with NYSE and Nasdaq for international IPO business; he also launched and served on the board of Aim, working with regional and national legal and accounting firms to promote this successful growth companies market. After this, he became managing director of Jaffe Europe, working with a wide range of law, accounting, and consulting firms, largely on client relationship and satisfaction programs. Moving in-house, he led the marketing functions of BSI Management Systems, a global certification body, and international law firm Taylor Wessing LLP.

Based in New York since 2008, he is currently director of business development (global shared services) at Alvarez & Marsal LLC, a global professional services firm best known for restructuring and performance improvement. He is also an associate of the Z/Yen Group. He has designed and implemented over 10 key relationship programs in accounting, law, and consulting firms.

Robert is a graduate of Oxford University where he majored

in history. He has an MBA (distinction) from Cass Business School, City University, London; he holds a UK Market Research Society Diploma (distinction); and is a certified business coach. He is fluent in French, German, and Spanish.

He is contactable at robert@robertpayconsulting.com or via www.robertpayconsulting.com.

Susan Pettit is the founder and managing director of Client Central, and has been helping businesses create profitable client relationships for over 16 years. Working with a range of high-profile professional services firms as well as a leading international research company, Susan has a unique perspective on how to undertake and manage client listening programs. She has presented on the subject of client feedback around the world, contributed to leading business publications, and works hand in hand with her clients to ensure they extract maximum value from each and every feedback project undertaken. For more information visit clientcentral.co.uk.

Deepa Vargis-Tharmaraj, currently a legal director for Middle East, Africa, and Turkey at Dell FZ-LLC, a leading enterprise and consumer technology solutions provider, is responsible for providing legal advice on all matters supporting the local and regional Dell businesses. She joined Dell four years ago, having previously worked at British Telecom in roles involving intellectual property, product development (patent licensing, technology transfer, and collaborations), and procurement. She is also the telecom, media, and technology sector lead for the Association of Corporate Counsel, Middle East. Within Dell, Deepa is the global program manager to one of Dell's 11 employee resource groups (a CSR initiative) that focuses on connecting cultures and celebrating diverse perspectives – Mosaic. Deepa is also passionate about innovation and inspiring the next generation within the UAE to be bold and take on new challenges. She has embraced social media and actively speaks and writes about innovation in the UAE and beyond. She is also a committee member of the GCC national committee for an international network of not-for-profit schools, United World College.

Ian Turvill is the chief marketing officer of Freeborn & Peters LLP, a full-service law firm and GGI member headquartered in Chicago. Ian oversees the firm's marketing and business development functions, including marketing strategy, marketing communications, digital media, public relations, and client events and outreach. Ian is the treasurer-elect of the international Legal Marketing Association. He is a graduate of the University of Oxford and was also a John M. Olin Fellow at the Simon School of Business. He has dual US/UK citizenship.

Jill Weber is chief marketing and business development officer for Stinson Leonard Street, where she created Fast Forward®, a nationally recognized revenue program. Jill appears on the *National Law Journal*'s "50 Business of Law Trailblazers & Pioneers" and was recognized as an "Unsung Legal Hero" by *Minnesota Lawyer*. She has received 22 local and national Legal Marketing Association (LMA) "Your Honor" awards. She will be the 2017 president of the LMA board of directors, and attended Harvard Law School's "Leadership in Law Firms" executive education program.

Part 1:
Insight and Practice

Chapter 1: **Aligning strategy, culture, and performance management with a growth agenda**

By Andrew Hedley, director of Hedley Consulting Ltd.

Sustainable revenue growth is central to the longer term success of any firm. Strategies which underpin such growth, a client-centric culture that recognizes its importance, and an approach to performance management which encourages and rewards the behaviors that deliver growth are the triumvirate which form our subject matter. It is by aligning all three that firms provide the best opportunity for enduring success.

The market remains challenging for many; while activity is certainly on the rise, pressure on price is unabated. In simple terms, the savvy client wants the work done better, faster, and cheaper than it was last year. Firms are having to run faster to stand still. For the first time ever in the legal sector, increased activity on the clock is not translating to commensurate revenue growth on the top line.

Those businesses which can adapt to this new paradigm, by enhancing both their revenue generation and operating models, may be able to preserve profit but others will find themselves simply running faster to stand still.

The growth imperative

Growth is fundamental to longer term, sustainable success for any business in a competitive environment. "If you're not growing you're going backwards" is a phrase often heard which, from a business development perspective, carries much weight in a world where relative competitive strength is key to securing, developing, and retaining both clients and people.

.ncremental cost-base rises are inevitable, even in a low-inflation environment, and in the absence of matching revenue growth can only be paid for through reduced profit. Moreover, in order to compete effectively, firms need to do much more than simply repair and renew their infrastructures – they need to invest in people, technology, premises, and infrastructure. This can only be done in a way which is not profit-eroding through a healthy and rising top line.

Looked through the eyes of the client, a firm which is growing can be seen to offer many advantages both practically and psychologically. Growth will often be associated with increased resources, wider practice lines, increased geographic footprint, and an enhanced approach to service. All of these factors offer tangible benefits to clients, whether by servicing existing work better or providing the potential to support future expansion. At an emotional level, clients enjoy the halo effect of being associated with a successful firm. It reinforces that they have made a good choice and that their lawyers have a robust position within the legal services market.

Similarly, higher growth will be associated with increased opportunities for staff, and having a rising star brand on one's CV is a positive outcome. In a market in which the war for talent is intense, being an attractive employer brand, one seen to be going places, has a material impact on the nature of the candidates attracted to the firm. This begets a virtuous circle – better people, providing enhanced service, leading to more satisfied clients more inclined to place more work with the firm, so driving growth further.

The right sort of growth also drives profit per equity partner ("PEP") in a way which is sustainable. In the low growth period that followed the great recession, we saw firms reducing partner numbers in order to preserve PEP at acceptable levels. The nature of any law firm, with very high fixed costs, means that profit is very highly leveraged by top line growth. Once costs are covered any incremental increase in revenue falls straight to the bottom line, significantly increasing the overall profit pool. The converse is also true; until those high fixed costs are covered no profit flows at all.

Strategic overview – The nature of growth

Simply to say, "We need to grow the top line" is misleading. It is important to understand underlying profit drivers and to differentiate between organic and inorganic growth. This will ensure that the quality of any revenue increase is understood, and that different ways of working are considered strategically.

At its core, strategy is centered on the creation of a sustainable competitive advantage. The way in which a business goes about achieving this will vary from firm to firm but there are three key drivers of profitable growth that should be borne in mind.

To grow its top line a firm must either sell more "units" of legal services or be able to charge more per unit (of course, combining the two options is an additional third route). There are, quite simply, no other options. These routes will all necessarily result in growth and profit.

Looking at the volume of business sold, a firm can encourage existing clients to buy more of its services, seek out clients who are not users of legal services and convert them, or acquire new business by acquiring the work currently done by other firms, i.e. implement strategies to grow the client base by acquiring other firms' clients. This can be achieved from within its existing resources by winning pitches and converting prospective clients or by "acquiring" clients through inorganic means, which is discussed in more detail below.

Assuming a steady pricing and operating model, additional profit will flow when the cost of processing a "unit" diminishes (through a better utilization of overhead) and occasionally will be reduced as additional productive capacity needs to be created (hiring more staff, better systems, etc.) in order to service the work that has been generated.

In seeking growth, firms need to be clear about three separate but related issues:

1. Is the growth organic or inorganic?
2. Maintaining an eye to quality as well as quantity; and
3. Are we seeking to run the same race faster or to run a different race?

Organic or inorganic?

At its most fundamental, growth can be organic or inorganic.

Organic growth refers to growth that is delivered by the business as it stands, without any M&A activity or determined program of lateral hiring. It will be accompanied by an increase in productivity, as outlined above, and so the delivery of enhanced profits. The same asset base will process more revenue. Revenue per partner will rise without the need to cull partners. From this rise in revenue a leveraged increase in profit will be enjoyed.

Inorganic growth refers to a range of activity from outright M&A, through team moves to a strategy founded in multiple lateral hires. With varying degrees of certainty, they provide the opportunity to deliver step change uplifts in turnover but do not come without challenges of their own. These will often relate to culture, integration, and the discovery (in anything but a full merger) that the portability of a client base is not so straightforward as one might assume. Clients are inherently "sticky" to their incumbent firms and, where those firms have implemented sensible policies to institutionalize relationships, can be disinclined to move their business elsewhere.

Such growth can also serve to better sweat the firm's pre-existing assets and so deliver excellent marginal profitability. Adding a lateral partner into an office in which a desk, IT infrastructure, and support services already exist means that the marginal additional overhead is negligible.

An eye to quality as well as quantity

In evaluating the business sustainability of the growth that has been achieved it is important to look at productivity factors

– such as revenue per partner and revenue per lawyer – in addition to revenue increases. It is only by driving productivity that growth can be sustainably translated into enhanced profitability. Any firm wishing to both retain its existing high-performers and attract others of a similar ilk, able to take it to the next level, must demonstrate good growth metrics and a positive trend line.

The quality of any increased revenue also needs to be understood; it is an oft-quoted phrase that "turnover is vanity and profit is sanity". It would be senseless and ultimately terminal for the firm to "buy" work through pricing which means that it cannot be processed in a way which both meets client expectations and delivers an acceptable return for the firm. As an aside, the third element of this phrase – "cash is reality" – is not often spoken but it should also feature large in the thinking of firms, especially those in sectors with significant lock up and where funding the work that has just been won could have quite major implications.

Running the same race faster or running a different race?

One of strategy guru Michael Porter's most famous sayings is that operational effectiveness is not strategy. Operational effectiveness, he contends, is about running the same race better or faster. Strategy, on the other hand, is about running a different race.

That is not to say that operational effectiveness is not critical. Nor that the vast majority of firms need to undertake significant strides in this area if they are to be sustainable in even the short term. Rather, it is making that point that ultimately, in a competitive market, operational effectiveness is a zero sum game. Simply being more operationally effective may create a short term advantage but, with the passage of time, such gains will be eroded by competitors – either through imitation or leap-frogging with operational changes of their own.

So operational efficiency may indeed result in a growth and profit spike, but without a more considered and strategic approach this is unlikely to be sustainable.

Exploring strategic options and choices

The pursuit of revenue growth is most likely to succeed when it is underpinned by a clear strategy which allows resources to be directed to those areas most likely to deliver the strongest returns. This should be self-evident, but there are still many examples of firms pursuing scatter-gun approaches which generate much activity without commensurate results.

Positioning and Ansoff's generic strategies

The elegant simplicity of Ansoff's product/market matrix is often underappreciated. By distilling marketing strategy down into four generic options, a framework is created which allows decision making to be undertaken with precision and clarity.

An adapted version of the matrix (using a services/client notation) is shown in Figure 1, which has been supplemented to reflect the market challenges faced by those selling intangible services with a high knowledge content (in this context, legal services).

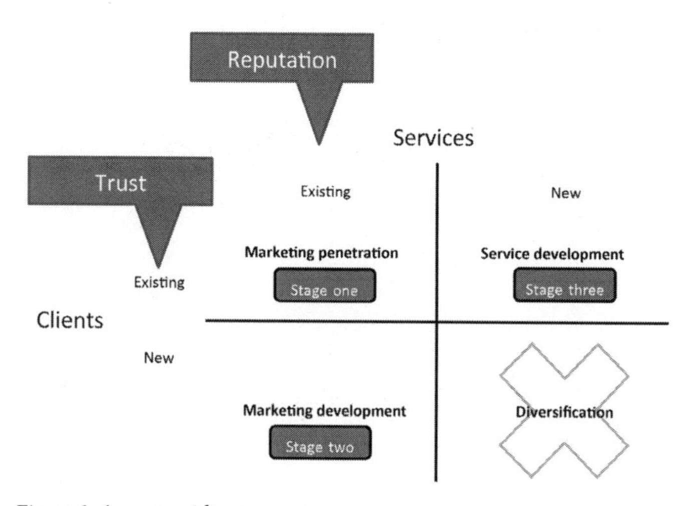

Figure 1: A services/clients matrix

Proposed by Igor Ansoff in *Corporate Strategy*,[1] it suggests that any business has four fundamental marketing strategies that it can pursue, based around existing and new clients or markets together with existing and new services. The four fundamental marketing strategies may be summarized as:

- **Market penetration** – Sell more existing services to existing clients;
- **Market development** – Sell existing services to new clients;
- **Service development** – Sell new services to existing clients; and
- **Diversification** – Sell new services to new clients.

This sequence also represents the approach that should be adopted to give the best likelihood of success.

Stage one is market penetration. Assuming that there is good satisfaction with existing services among existing clients, it is far easier to expand sales here than to try to break new ground elsewhere.

Interestingly, the Ansoff matrix also predicts that it will be easier to sell existing services (for which one has reputation, track record, and market position) to non-clients than to sell new services to existing ones (in which trust may be high but could be outdone by the perceived risk of making a decision to purchase an unproven service). In other words, market development should be prioritized above service development as stages two and three.

The challenge of selling a new service to a new client (i.e. diversification) in sufficiently significant volumes to make a difference to the top line in any substantive way is recognized as being a slow-burn strategy. Within marketing planning, which typically has a 12-month horizon, such diversification activities are not even considered – they are on the longer term business planning agenda. This is a stage four activity.

Client retention and growth

Having reflected on these generic strategies it is unsurprising that sophisticated firms place huge emphasis on client retention, the deepening of existing service lines, and the introduction of new practice capabilities.

This may be manifested by key account programs which focus on only a select number of high-importance clients, but should always be underpinned by a philosophy which places the client at the center of all activities and builds a service model on the basis of what is best for them rather than most convenient for the firm.

Sales pursuit

An excellent retention strategy does not remove the need to replenish the client base with new blood. However, the acquisition of new business should be targeted and consider questions such as:

- What is the competitive context – which will impact on our probability of success and the prices that we can charge?
- How profitable will the work be? Can we use existing capabilities or will investment be required?
- Does the client have an ongoing requirement for legal services or is it likely to be a highly episodic relationship? What is our view on the lifetime value of the client?
- Are there opportunities to introduce additional service lines? Over what timescale?
- What is the cost of sales? How long will it take us to recover this sunk cost? What is the opportunity-cost of pursuing this client versus others?

These are all questions which prompt a more considered approach to ensure that one of any law firm's scarcest resources, the way in which its people use their time, is invested in ways that deliver the best results.

Pricing strategy and robust financial hygiene

Pricing is a critical component of the revenue growth equation. In addition to agreeing the overall pricing for a particular piece of work, there is also the issue of maintaining good financial hygiene through the life of a matter. As we have seen, small decreases at the top line have a leveraged effect on the bottom line. It follows that revenue growth can be enhanced in practical terms by focusing hard on pricing and improving negotiation skills, together with better matter management.

Pricing for law firms is increasingly market based. Understanding the market in which they are operating is key if pricing decisions are to be optimal – profit or loss is made at the margin with too few partners appreciating that even a fee discount of five percent will erode profit significantly. If a firm's margin is 30 percent then a 5 percent price cut has the effect of reducing profit by around 17 percent.

What this means in practical terms in many firms is that those who negotiate the fee (generally the partner with the client relationship) need to be much more conversant with negotiation techniques and have a clearer understanding of their firm's key price points at which profit is made or eroded. They also need a good working picture of the competitive market for the work that is being negotiated.

It is also not uncommon for firms to triple or quadruple discount their fees – once in the initial negotiation, again by not tracking variances for which an additional fee would be payable, next by inaccurately recording their inputs (i.e. time) for work which is chargeable on that basis, and finally by making value judgments as to how much time will be recoverable at the point of raising an invoice and under-billing at that point. Given that such leakage can only come off the profit line, it is surprising how few law firm partners are focused seriously and determinedly on these areas.

A further pricing trend is the move towards fixed fees for particular types of work. The profit equation then moves to the issue of internal efficiency. Revenue growth, in these circumstances, is determined by deciding on the correct price point to meet demand and increase unit sales. In a market where most legal services are poorly differentiated and brands are weak, this is very challenging. The position is exacerbated by the high levels of price transparency afforded by new technologies, the internet, social media, and clients' sharing of pricing data through trade forums and the media. In common with all businesses, when perceived differentiation between competing offers is low, decisions tend to be price driven.

There are significant opportunities for the marketer to support pricing through effective brand positioning strategies, genuine added value differentiation (on dimensions which are important to the client) and through the creation of a high trust relationship between client and firm that will support more robust pricing.

Culture and performance management

There is an important cultural dimension to any growth agenda. This needs to be underpinned with a performance management approach which encourages and rewards the sorts of activities and behaviors that are most likely to lead to profitable revenue growth.

Cultures which encourage sustainable growth are founded in a deep concern for the client and a desire to assist them in achieving success. This is, of course, at odds with the view of the sales person as a parasite interested only in making the sale. There is no place for characters of this nature in any walk of life, and certainly not the professions. Research into the nature of the most effective sales people demonstrates that they have a deep concern for their clients. They also have a strong desire to make the sale but always within the context of what is best for the client. This is how enduring relationships are built.

A performance management approach which employs a balanced scorecard to evaluate both leading and lagging indicators of success will help to ensure that client focus is maintained. It will also encourage the culture and behaviors needed to ensure that a growth mentality is nurtured and developed.

By having clarity on such issues the firm will encourage those with the required skill sets and attitudes to fulfil their potential, as well as attracting others of the same mind set. The corollary will also be true; those who do not organize themselves around their clients' needs, or who fail to appreciate the importance of growth to the sustainability of the firm, will find themselves at odds with its strategic journey and will most likely vote with their feet.

The recipe for growth

Having a well-founded strategy is vital to ensure that growth is targeted, profitable, and sustainable. This is, however, only part of the equation. The strategy sets out the intellectual case, ensures robust analysis, and produces a road map, but it is the people who give it effect. This is why culture and performance management are also vital ingredients in the overall recipe for growth.

Taken together, they are the three foundation stones of success. Each can create a positive effect on its own, but the true synergies are only realized when all are aligned to create a multiplier effect which maximizes any firm's growth potential.

Reference

1. Ansoff, H. I., *Corporate Strategy: An Analytic Approach to Business Policy for Growth and Expansion*, New York: McGraw-Hill, 1965.

Chapter 2:
Designing a key relationship program – Getting started and process overview

By Robert Pay, director of business development (global shared services) at Alvarez & Marsal

Why a key relationship program?

A "key relationship program" (KRP) or "key account program" should form the bedrock of any law firm's growth strategy. Law firms have generally been laggards or have only superficially adopted relationship programs, so this is a technique that has real competitive advantage.

For some law firms, clients represent a marketplace of one, with the largest companies spending several hundred million dollars a year on professional services, demanding an organized and tailored approach to build business. Getting 10 percent more work from a few major clients can dwarf the returns on developing scores of new relationships, with much less effort. It is generally recognized to be easier to sell to people with whom you already have relationships. Conversely, losing a major client can impact the firm's bottom line in a dramatic way. Keeping what you have is a prerequisite to a growth strategy.

A key relationship program is a systematic effort to grow and sustain those clients and referral sources that really impact the bottom line of a firm; relationships that have the potential to be important future clients, either by virtue of their growth or the capacity for the firm to grow its relationships, may also be included. The differences between the traditional partnership model for dealing with clients and a formal program are shown in Table 1.

This chapter covers the principal elements of a program, how to set about the design and assemble the teams necessary to manage the design, and the factors that increase acceptance of the concept of relationship management. It also includes a questionnaire to test your readiness for the introduction of a program, and it concludes with a section on typical barriers to the successful implementation of a program and some remedies.

Traditional client approach	Client relationship management
Intuitive	Intuition plus process, learning, and technology
Service levels at individual partners' discretion	Firm service levels, plus clients' individual service objectives, clearly defined
Client relationships proprietary	Client relationships belong to the partnership
Role of partners vis-à-vis client relationships undefined	Roles of partners and lawyers defined; performance measured and rewarded
Little focus on individual client relationships by firm management	Firm management monitors the progress of important relationships
No planning or client prioritization. No assessment of future work pipeline	Identification and analysis of the firm's major clients; individual client action plans
Informal reviews	Formal reviews

Table 1: Comparison of a traditional approach and client relationship management

Preconditions for successful adoption of a KRP

A KRP demands a level of behavioral change, and certain preconditions are necessary in order to hardwire the process to the firm's culture – i.e. change the way things are done until it becomes second nature. It is because we need to address behavioral change that a truly multi-disciplinary approach is required to design a KRP: human resources (rewards); training (skills); technology (CRM systems); finance (information flows); as well as business development/marketing.

In order for a change to be adopted successfully, three things have to be in place. Partners need to:

- Want to change – There needs to be a "burning platform", the desire to do better or arrest decline or to overtake the competition (this is largely a job for firm leadership);
- Be able to change – Have the skills, infrastructure, and support necessary; and
- Be allowed to change – Sometimes rules change but the culture says, "Don't worry about that, do as I do". When a change is introduced, non-partners will look to see if the partners take it seriously, and the partners will look to see if the high performers comply.

It is a truism that what gets measured is far more likely to get done. One of the key factors in designing a successful KRP is judging the level of input required by the frontline professionals and ensuring that there are performance-monitoring rewards, and possible sanctions. There is no doubt that you need to get the firm or local/practice area management fully behind the initiative and to build a robust coalition.

Getting buy-in for the concept

The person responsible for introducing the concept of a KRP could be a chief marketing officer (CMO), managing partner, or a head of practice area or region. Whether a program is aimed at the whole firm, a single practice area, or an office, country, or region, you are dealing with behavioral change and to ensure the concept is fully understood requires building a coalition. This is normally achieved by making a business case based on a combination of business imperatives that are most likely to resonate with your management team (see Table 2).

Possible reasons for implementing a key relationship program	
Category	***Details***
Financial	• Focus best resource on the best opportunities (scale/profitability) • Reducing cost of sales, reducing need to pitch for new work • Improve the nature of work undertaken • Increase the volume of work undertaken
Competitor advantage	• Become better placed for opportunities than competition • Improved chances of winning new business
Risk management	• Stem attrition by focusing on valuable relationships at risk • Institutionalize relationships against defections and competitors • Reduce exposure to large clients or a single industry • Decrease dependence on a few key rainmaker client partners
Cultural	• Improve transparency and accountability for precious assets • Develop a client-centered, business development culture
Insurance	• Protection against downward fee pressure • Mitigate damage of service shortfalls

Table 2: Benefits of a relationship management approach

Draw up a compelling business case

The project leader for the program should develop a straw man, citing factors militating against a KRP and based on discussions with frontline professionals, observations, as well as hard data of client attrition. (This assumes that the firm monitors client loss and conducts exit interviews to understand why they left.) It is worth spending a few weeks making the case to ensure full buy-in. Where the case for the KRP is not compelling, the speed and degree of uptake is reduced, impacting the overall success of the program and possibly requiring a re-launch.

It may be helpful for the concept champions to review the culture and the current policies and to ask the following questions:

- What impact does our current remuneration and client allocation system have on encouraging or discouraging people to cooperate and grow client business?
- How good are our firm's client-facing activities and relationship building? And, perhaps most importantly
- What will the attitude of our people be to this idea?

The initial backing of both the management team and front-line leadership is critical. If the program changes the nature of being a client partner and their remuneration, this can only really be addressed at management level. (A section on barriers and some suggestions on how to deal with them follows at the end of this chapter.) Once the senior management team has bought in to the concept, get a mandate to start designing your program. Of course, you may do this at an office, industry group, or country level, but that may limit your ability to change firm processes and policies. Some programs emerge from a single practice or country and become firm programs.

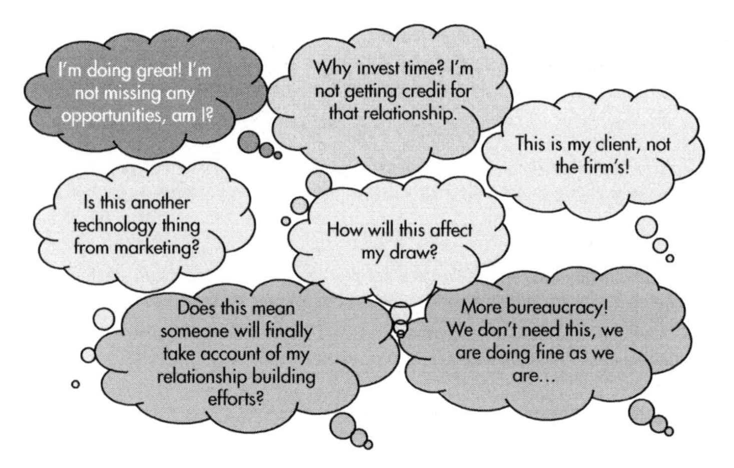

Figure 1: Mind map on barriers to a KRP

The design process

While it is possible to truncate the process of developing the program and not every detail of what is covered in this chapter is essential, it is critical to:

- Work out the rationale for undertaking the program and its objectives;
- Create a team of people to drive the program and design the process;
- Develop some tools and documents to capture intelligence and drive action;
- Devise a set of metrics to measure progress and motivate action; and
- Communicate effectively within the firm about the program.

This ignores any training and skills development, which lie beyond the remit of the BD function in many firms. Work with what you have to get the process going.

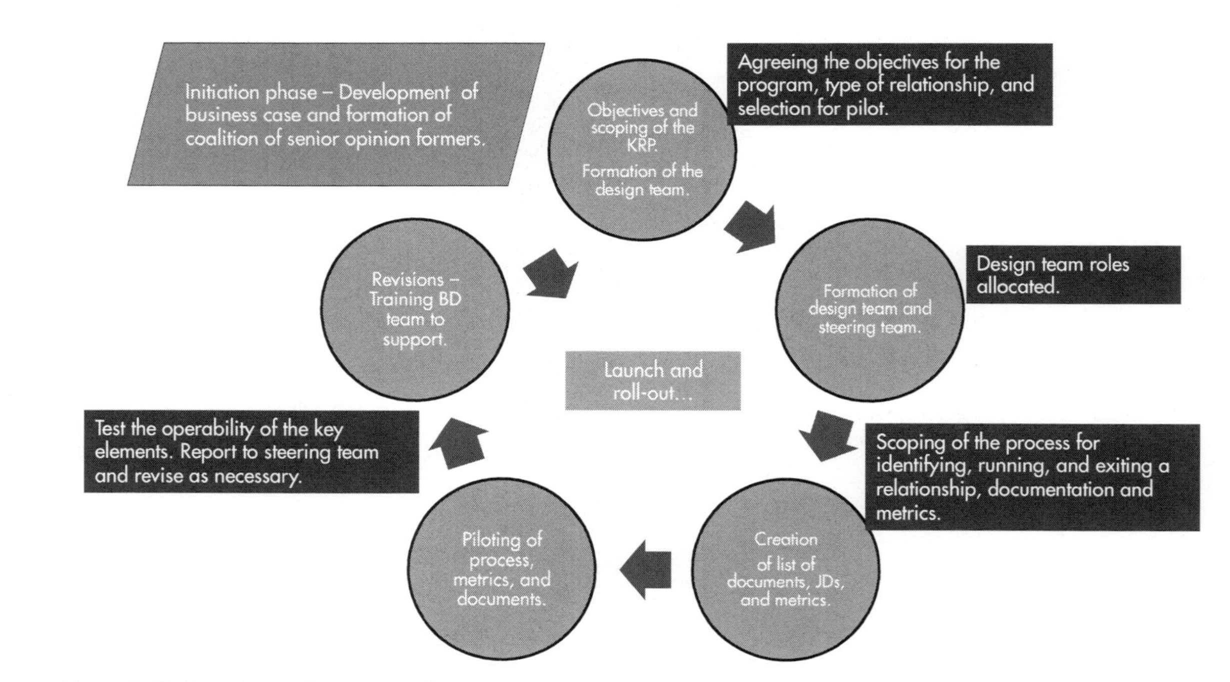

Figure 2: The key relationship program design process overview

Setting the program objectives

There may be a "burning platform" for your program: rapid client attrition, or a widely recognized need to get deeper into relationships to avoid becoming a commodity adviser or dropping perilously low on a panel. For many law firms, pressure on routine work has led them to focus on higher margin work. (This is not only a relationship issue; the ability to work "smarter" through technology has impacted on where work gets done, with some work moving in house or being done by lower-skilled lawyers or paralegals.)

In most firms, however, the need may not be that obvious, so a crucial first step is to develop a compelling rationale for the project. This should reference all pertinent issues to the firm/practice area or office/region or country, and illustrate the business case for the program. The type of information might include:

- Attrition rates;
- Exposure to large clients – and impact of client loss;
- Impact of adding X number of new clients over a specific billing threshold;
- Impact on the bottom line of increasing billing to the largest 10 clients by X percent;
- Examples of where individuals have introduced other service lines and successfully grown business;
- Competitor information – illustrations of well-run competitors eating into major clients, etc.

Relationship program design team

Process overview

There are many moving parts in a KRP, but these can generally be broken down into the following broad headings: design; and building relationships.

Design

- **Scope** – Which relationships should be in your KRP; how are they selected and rejected? Should these relationships have a different status to other relationships? How will they be removed?
- **People and process** – Who should run the relationships, team structure, roles and responsibilities, performance reviews, and rewards? How do we change?
- **Information and documentation** – What information do we need to capture? What information is useful for running the relationships? How do we analyze client relationships and develop a common vocabulary for the program? And
- **Metrics** – What do we measure and how, both for the relationships and the performance of the client teams and individuals? How can we get engagement on an ongoing basis? How do we refresh the constituents of the program?

Building relationships

- **Building relationships** – How can we best build relationships in this firm? What does "good" look like in this firm?
- **Service** – Are we providing the right services in the way the client wants them? How do we improve value and satisfaction?
- **Social media and relationships** – With many business executives having an online presence, might we use social media to enhance relationships? And
- **Technology** – How do we make intelligent use of technology to support relationship management?

It is hard to disentangle these topics from each other, but the above list makes a useful agenda from which to drive a program specific to your firm. It may not make sense to address them all at once; for example, refreshing the program is not as urgent as getting initial engagement and working out how to drive the behaviors that support building more profitable relationships.

The success of a program will be in the frontline; therefore, it is essential to design each element to suit the frontline and the firm's culture. Programs that start with, and are owned by, the marketing function will probably have less likelihood of gaining traction. While a professional – probably the CMO, a senior BD person, or specialist consultant – will undertake all the heavy lifting in terms of creating the tools, a team is necessary to help tune the program to the culture.

As an illustration, the requirement for a formal third-party debrief with the client after a major transaction or a set period might be a "must do" for one firm and a "nice to do" in another. Basic communication issues such as documentation format may be important, too. Consulting businesses tend to prefer PowerPoint and Excel to Word documents, and they prefer shorthand and color coding. Law firms have a tendency towards text and want Word documents. The degree of documentation or the frequency of review meetings, for example, might be something that derails the program.

A relationship program "design team" is a useful way to tune the KRP to the firm's culture. This is normally a trinity of: a core team, comprising dedicated or nearly full time members, charged with driving the project and creating processes and documentation; a halo team, comprising frontline users and specialists; and an overall steering group to which the project reports.

Category	Key items
People	• Client team roles and responsibilities; • Roles for management team; • Performance metrics and rewards; and • When and how to transition or change a client partner.
Documentation	• Job descriptions; • Relationship action plan; • Guidance and expectations for running a client team; and • Guidelines on relationship building.
Processes and policies	• Status of a client in the program – call on resources, etc; • When to undertake a service review (scale of transaction or frequency); • Client-facing skills development; • Provision of reports to team leaders; • Reviews of client partners; and • What information should be logged for key clients in the system.
Metrics	• Setting of goals for specific clients; • Financial metrics, growth objectives, etc; • Client satisfaction – informal interview protocols, etc; and • Key service attributes to be measured.
Communications	• Developing a common vocabulary around the program, e.g. relationship strength; • Naming of the program and relationships – key, core, or platinum; • Names of roles – client partner, relationship partner, team leader; and • Promoting best practice.

Table 3: Example of elements of a key relationship program

Core design team

The first step is to create a small, "core" design team to design the program and all the elements (see Table 3). The composition of the team is important for getting buy-in. It is critical that the team contains people who are credible business developers, and who are respected by the partners as such. Ideally, one of these should be the mouthpiece or public face of the program, preferably a star rainmaker.

The managing partner or chief executive should also be involved, but not act as the spokesperson unless they are or were credible relationship builders. The core team might also include someone senior from HR if you are contemplating changing compensation or introducing a training program to support behavioral change.

As some of your most skilled rainmakers may be skeptical of process, they may not support the program, and indeed may undermine it by not participating (or worse). For this reason, it might be useful to include such a skeptic in the team, albeit one who is not so hostile as to be disruptive. This process will hopefully convert them, and they often see and proselytize the benefits for the firm as a whole.

Halo design team – User group

While you might have a small core design team to get things done fast, you might have a wider "halo team" that reflects all the disciplines that are likely to play a role in making your program work. The idea is to get input at the design stage, and also to give the program a sense of ownership. This might include:

- Frontline and middle-ranking professionals with known BD talents;
- Support staff: IT, finance, and HR, training, and business development managers; and
- Project manager to keep the project on track.

The support staff may be allocated specific issues related to their discipline. For example, the HR member to look at changes in the performance review documentation or rewards, or the finance member to ensure that billing information for a specific client can be aggregated and sent to the client. It is a real barrier if your finance system organizes data around matters and not around clients, or has difficulty in recognizing subsidiary businesses as part of a group. This seems a common problem in law firms. Having someone focus on a workaround early on in the process can save post-launch disappointment when client team leaders find that they cannot get billing information, depriving them of an overview of the relationship's finances.

A project manager is particularly useful, given that everybody involved will have a day job. Most consulting firms have access to these skill sets, and if there is no one from BD then IT may be able to provide a resource. For a smaller firm or a practice area, a competent CMO, senior manager, or specialist consultant will be able to take responsibility for the project management as part of their design role.

The relationship program steering group

A steering group is a way of getting the firm's senior management involved, and this is desirable for two reasons. First, you need support at the top for the program, just as you would for the roll-out of a new performance process and remuneration policy or for a new billing system. Secondly, when it comes to evaluation of performance of the program and the team leaders, this is likely to be carried out above the pay grade of the chief marketing officer. There may also be other political issues that require senior involvement, such as when clients may need to be exited from the program, either because the relationship has failed to the extent that it is no longer defensible or because the client's business trajectory does not warrant the status of being in the KRP. This is particularly the case where a KRP relationship status has greater command of resource than a regular client.

On the basis that what is measured matters, it is useful to have an annual review of each relationship by this senior steering group. The amount of time required may be significant, though one may ask what could be more important. The membership of this group might include not only firm management, but also regional management, and particularly industry group heads relevant to the relationship. One of the benefits of involving this level of person is that they provide the opportunity to spread insights around the firm, sharing good practice and passing on ideas. This may be happening within industry groups and practice areas, but it is a feature of partnerships that good ideas often remain stubbornly isolated when they might be recycled for the benefit of other clients. Finally, it might require senior people to resolve issues around team leadership and team membership.

Launching the concept

Ideally, the concept of the program should be launched to influential partners – say, the management board – before going to the wider partnership and the frontline. Senior support is critical to success, even if some of the most enthusiastic supporters are often younger partners and senior managers on the partnership track. A presentation at a partners' conference is highly recommended if they are not familiar with the idea of a KRP.

For wider consumption, the design team should draw up a statement of intent or mission statement for the project, setting out briefly the rationale for the project. This initial communication should come from the firm leadership (managing partner or chief executive) and the public face of the program (if they are not the same people).

A useful interim step is to consider a survey to gauge the appetite or resistance to the idea of a program in general or to test specific issues, such as the willingness to allow third parties to interview clients. The results and feedback from such a survey can help to identify resistance points or misunderstandings, or improve the way you connect.

Key relationship management self-diagnostic

This questionnaire has been designed to gauge the extent to which your firm can be said to have a key relationship management program. There are three sections:

1. Your firm's current program;
2. Your firm's culture and its capability for a program; and
3. Your BD/marketing department's capacity to support a relationship program.

For each of the following questions please use a cross to indicate the statement that ***best*** describes your view. Please choose ***only one*** statement from each question.

CURRENT STATUS	Check	Score
1. Which of the following statements best describes your firm's approach to a key relationship program?		
a. Individual partners are assumed to be responsible for developing their clients. There is no formal key relationship program.		0
b. We have a program with a list of member organizations and teams, but not much else is written down or measured.		2
c. We have a program with teams, live plans and roles and responsibilities clearly laid out.		3
d. In addition to (c) we measure the results of our program internally and validate the status of our relationships with the clients/referral sources.		5

2. If you have a KRP, what is the level of adherence?		
a. People ignore it or pay lip service...		1
b. Uptake is patchy, but there are some areas of the firm that really get it...		2
c. There are a few naysayers, but by and large everyone gets it and follows the disciplines...		3
d. It is the way things get done; it is part of the culture, and of what gets measured, and how individual performance is evaluated.		4
SUITABILITY FOR A KRP		
3. Which statement best reflects the current culture of your firm regarding a client partner involving others?		
a. Some people cross-refer and team because it is the right thing to do, though the reward system encourages a proprietorial approach to clients.		1
b. There is a patchy level of cooperation between many partners dependent on personal good will.		2
c. We have a few barriers to cooperation on major client relationships and the management supports and incentivizes sharing of relationships.		3
d. We have analyzed and removed barriers to cooperation on client work and ensured that our reward system incentivizes teamwork.		3

4. Your BD/marketing function		
Which statement best reflects the role of your current marketing/BD team? *(Check only one box)*		
a. Our BD/marketing function is very centralized and focuses mainly on marketing communications and writing proposals and has little involvement with specific client relationships.		1
b. BD managers sit in each division/ service line and support a wide range of general BD/marketing with a limited involvement in client relationships.		2
c. Our BD function plays a support role to client teams organizing internal meetings, events, updating client action plans, and inputting data into the CRM system.		3
d. Our BD function has significant involvement in meetings and planning around key relationships and makes a significant contribution to strategy.		4
5. Appetite for/attitudes towards a KRP		
Which statement best reflects the culture of your firm? *(Check only one box)*		
a. Our firm does really well through the innate skills and historic structural capital (brand name client base). We don't need a special program; client relationship management is in our DNA.		0
b. We think what we are doing currently is fine, but we do need more rigor or process.		1

c. The focus on relationship management and client focus in general needs to improve as our competitors are getting better at this.		2
d. The management team is committed to driving client focus though client relationship and service initiatives.		3
e. We use third parties to interview our clients to measure the strength of relationships/client satisfaction, etc.		4
6. Your most senior BD/marketing officer		
Which statement best reflects the culture of your firm? ***(Check every box that applies)***		
a. Is focused mainly on marketing communications (website/PR, etc.).		0
b. Designed and/or runs our key relationship program.		3
c. We have another professional who is responsible on a day-to-day basis for our relationship program (head of business development).		2
d. Is a lawyer or a journalist who moved into marketing/BD.		0
e. Is someone who would be credible in person meeting our most important clients.		2
f. Has extensive marketing/BD experience in business and/or multiple professions (other than this one) and has designed or run KRPs elsewhere.		3

What your score means...

Maximum score: 30

Your score 25 plus: You are part of a small elite group of firms. You probably only need to tighten up your process, for example by undertaking more third party interviews.

Your score 15–25: You are on the road to getting serious about a key relationship program.

Your score below 15: Your firm is in the danger zone or in profitable complacency.

Piloting

Avoid a "Big Bang" launch where you are unlikely to be able to support a multitude of relationships. It is advisable to start small, with a pilot group. It is very demanding to be working with new documentation and concepts while trying to shape them to your firm. A pilot with a small number of relationships enables the design team to get really involved and also tends to energize the members of the pilot teams, knowing that they are in a vanguard and creating an important business process for the firm.

The heart of a program must be intelligent analysis of individual relationships and a team of people agreeing about whom, and on what, to focus your limited time and resources, and how best to improve the nature of the relationship. The best way to get started is to take a very small number of relationships: no more than four. You have the choice of taking four similar relationships or trying to better represent the firm's clients by selecting clients from different practice areas or locations. Another way would be to select based on risk criteria. Saving an "at risk" relationship would be a great way to launch – but it may also be risky! As this is the start of something new, playing it safe may make the most sense. It is probably advisable to choose relationships that are widely known in the firm and

	KRP Project Plan	**May**	**June**	**July**
1.	**Design phase**			
a.	Design team (DT) and steering group (SG)	x		
b.	Draft KRP documentation	◆━━◆ x		
c.	Develop process with design team	◆━━◆		
d.	Finalise Tier 1 (T1) and 2 (T2) relationship core teams	◆━━━	━━━◆	
e.	Beta test of four T1 relationships	◆━━━	◆	
f.	Executive committee review process		x	
2.	**Implementation trial phase**			
a.	Communications monthly update		x	x
b.	Release core documentation			
c.	Create action plans for all T1 and T2		◆━━━	━━━
d.	Develop guidelines for best practices with DT			◆━━━
e.	Program readiness and feedback survey			
f.	Design monitoring/metrics for performance			
g.	Pre-partner plan and team clean up alert to team leaders/team managers			
h.	Full launch, progress review, guidelines (partner meeting)			
3.	**Review and recalibration**			
a.	End of year relationship client team reviews			
b.			Complete	
			Underway	
			Imminent	
			Not started	

Figure 3: Sample KRP project plan

	August	September	October	November	December	
	x	x				
			x			
		x				
			x			
				x		

where you have team leaders who are likely to be competent. Saving underperforming partners is best reserved for later in the program.

Using these relationships as a test group, the design team should prioritize establishing the key elements of a relationship plan, a vocabulary to describe relationships, and draft roles for the client team. They should also work out the review process and key metrics, though these could come several months after the client teams are up and running. Anything that affects financial reward may take some time, while ensuring that performance is a review issue is normally fairly easy. Figure 3 is a worked example of a project plan.

Launch

During the pilot period, you can be identifying further client names and teams and training your BD team and/or team leaders and team managers in the process. As mentioned, it is a good idea to avoid a "Big Bang" launch with lots of client names and team leaders if you do not have the necessary time and resources to support them all in the short term.

There is a tendency for people to start querying lists and team members if the information is sent in a single communication. It is much better to announce names for inclusion in the relationship program once the team has already done its initial analysis and is underway. This also gives the program some new information on a regular basis. As we know, the financial rewards take some time, especially given the gestation period for clients to approve some major consulting projects. Relationships rarely turn on a dime.

A launch communication program could include:

- A cascade via practice groups or offices about the program – a figurehead respected by the firm as good at client relationship management, or the managing partner or CEO, make the best people to front the launch;

- Testimonials from teams involved on how they enhanced their approach to, and coordination of, the relationship (video or in person);
- Results in terms of improved understanding of relationships, internal liaison, opportunity spotting, and client billings; and
- Explanations of the process and documentation. BD people should lead this on the basis that if you can explain it you can support it. For BD personnel in generation 1.0 functions, this can help them deploy their skills where it will make a commercial difference.

The project leader should be responsible for collating comments and feedback from the launch for possible modifications.

Barriers to key relationship programs

Some firm cultures are particularly resistant to a concept that requires teamwork, transparency, and accountability to client work; up to this point, partners may have enjoyed total autonomy in their dealings with clients and have only been judged on their numbers. Table 4 shows the most common stumbling blocks to the introduction of systematic relationship management.

Complacency

Complacency about financial performance is less of an issue now than it was pre-crash. For the previous couple of decades, the earnings of many professional firms had risen in double digits annually, often without firms doing anything new or in any sense "working smarter". Client focus was often low down the list of priorities, while firms invested in the war for talent and IT infrastructure (including, ironically, expensive and underused CRM systems), or real estate.

Barriers to adoption of a KRP		
Barrier	**Characteristics**	**Issues for relationship management**
Complacency	Firm has been very successful relying on the natural skills of partners – possibly, this is a narrow cadre of rainmakers.	May be generational divisions with great client handlers having produced a cadre of technical partners. May be subject to client leakage and lost opportunities.
Remuneration	There may be some aspects of the remuneration that not only fail to promote openness but actually discourage it.	Only intuitively good client partners systematically grow relationships. Good guys get discouraged trying to grow work for others.
Client ownership	Management is not involved in client relationships. This may be related to the remuneration. Partners object to management oversight of how the relationship is run and developed.	Client partners hostile to the concept of a team involved in relationship development. Resistance to committing strategies to paper and third party client interviews.
Process resistance	People claim they are too busy to engage with the planning process.	Lack of documentation often implies a combination of no rigorous thought and/or no action. Makes progress hard to monitor.
Lack of program experience	Lack of experience, in the management team and support staff, of developing a KRP.	Increased likelihood of poor uptake and achieving objectives; probable need for re-launch or shelving of the program.

Table 4: Barriers to adoption of a KRP

Many firm websites are plastered with unsubstantiated claims about being "client-centered" or "client-focused" or "putting the client first" with no evidence that the firm even monitors their relationships or service quality. The main problem with this is that you may believe your own propaganda.

Remuneration policy

Remuneration policy is one of the most contentious and difficult aspects of a partnership to change, mainly because of the "winners and losers" effect. If a remuneration system treats partners like a collection of sole practitioners by rewarding them purely based on their own billings, there is likely to be a low level of cooperation in developing clients. Some natural "team players" may step up to the plate, but the culture will erode their goodwill and efforts. Naturally, there is a tendency for people to want to fill their own desk, and it is normally easiest to explain and sell what you have developed yourself. The opportunity cost in terms of money and relationships can be enormous.

The benefits for both the firm and individuals can be enormous if you redesign your remuneration system creatively to encourage teaming up on client relationships. The best approach is to start by agreeing what client management behaviors you want to encourage and, conversely, which current practices you want to discourage. The next step is to then test how well the current system promotes those desired outcomes and agree how it would need to change.

To avoid self-interest-skewing proposals, it would be best to use independent consultants to do this. Realistically, you may need to grandfather some in their existing reward structures while encouraging others to cooperate through bonus pools and/or more rapid promotion.

A law firm partner maintained his senior equity position by referring three times his own team's billings within the firm. This firm had designed its remuneration system to promote referral work. Interestingly, though, some partners often grumbled about his average personal numbers and his top of the equity position. Old mindsets die slowly.

In another law firm, a very successful partner was given two years to replicate his practice in another region. When he succeeded, the firm had a practice double the original size. Both partners had support in identifying target relationships, many already warm targets through contact with other practices.

In both cases, management gave the partners space and time to develop new business. It worked for the individuals and the firm. Flexing the system to accommodate relationship and business building prowess was a win-win. Giving partners goals to grow and develop relationships with individual clients can pay dividends.

Client ownership

No place for management?

Indeed, partners sometimes believe (as a matter of professional pride) that managing the client is the sole role of frontline professionals. In return, some management teams sometimes prefer just to look at figures to manage and reward their partners. It is also the case that managing partners are sometimes nervous of push-back against the idea of addressing something as private as a partner's personal client relationship. By contrast, the more engaged managing partners or chief executive officers are well aware of the state of major relationships; individual relationships will be discussed and senior management will be actively involved in building the relationship.

In one global firm where I implemented a KRP, the management team met in a different city every quarter. They wanted to show the partnership how seriously they took the program. As the regional executives met monthly in a different city, we decided that as an agenda item for each meeting, at least relationship team leaders from that city would give presentations on the health and prospects of the relationship for which they were responsible.

Resistance to client interviews

We cannot deal with the importance of client relationship and service metrics in detail in this chapter. Suffice it to say, however, that partners are often very reluctant to let someone else speak to their client about their satisfaction with the service they receive. Consider leaving this element until after the program is launched.

Process resistance

Too busy!

The continual cry of lack of time is hard to accept. Although there are busy times for all professionals, very few people are 100 percent billable, so the question remains – what do they do with their time that could be more important than focusing on key relationships? It is probably less time-consuming than chasing every new business opportunity that arises. In particular, very few New York law firms ever say no when invited to propose, regardless of the strength of relationship or number of other firms competing. There is a lot of time and resource wasted in business development in firms that do not have a KRP. As we will see, there is little "bureaucracy" required in running a program.

Rainmakers

The innate resistance or lack of participation from star rainmakers is one of the key reasons that some firms still do not have effective KRPs (or effective appraisal systems, for that matter). The leadership of such firms often comprises intuitively successful business developers who followed their own approach; unfortunately, these people may be among the most resistant to process.

As people with a natural gift, they often simply conclude that the real problem is that other partners are not like them. Some also enjoy their hallowed position as a star and may not wish to share the spotlight with too many others. Co-opt a big name partner into any KRP you are designing; have that person front it.

Lack of experience

Marketing functions

Designing a relationship program is one of the more complex marketing and business development activities. Whether your firm does or does not have the ability to set up a program often may reflect the way business development and marketing functions have developed.

Different firms and professions took different routes and chose different types of people to lead them. Some professions give preference to members of their own profession for senior marketing roles; in the US, major law firms often cite JD as a preferred qualification for a CMO. As a result, there is much less cross-fertilization between professions in the US than in Europe, and it is generally acknowledged that US law firms are further behind in adopting client relationship management. By contrast, accounting, consulting, and law in the rest of the English-speaking world, where people move frequently between these professions, adopted the technique in the 1980s and 1990s.

It may be instructive, in assessing your own readiness for a key relationship management program, to check if you require additional skills to design and implement a program. These

Roles	Model 1.0	Model 2.0	Model 3.0
Professional BD and marketing staff	Prime focus on brand building. May be outsourced: media relations, website, events, social media, etc.	Focus on business development support as well as brand building. Support partners in selling and RFPs.	Marketing professionals for communications. Large minority or majority focused on key relationships and key pursuits.
Partners	Do all the selling and all client contact unsupported.	Partners delegate some routine proposal writing to BD team.	Partners held accountable for key relationships and actively manage cross-firm client teams.
Minus →			Plus
Relationship management sophistication	Unsystematic: everything at the discretion of the partners. Relationships largely personal. Limited use of systems and technology on a firm basis.	Some identification of key relationship and paper client teams. No action plans and relationship maps – "it is all in our heads". A (little used) CRM system. Marketing activities have little deliberate focus on key relationships. Occasional client survey. Coalition of the willing means some relationships become institutional.	Client relationship program is understood across the firm. Non-partners involved. Regular surveying of key relationships – third party as well as team members. Client plans with clear objectives and programs of activity to grow the relationship. Relationships a management team issue. Aim to institutionalize clients.

Figure 4: The client-focused firm – What model does your firm most resemble?

skills can be transferred to the current team, providing they would have credibility talking about client relationships. Many BD professionals in professional firms have been consultants, investment bankers, or have worked in industries their firms are targeting, and so have experience servicing clients and selling assignments.

Chapter 3: **Let your clients be the guide to your strategic success**

By Susan Pettit, founder and managing director of Client Central

One of the most important decisions any law firm leader will have to make is which direction the firm's strategy should take.

For the purposes of illustration, let's discuss the challenges faced by a fictional managing partner of a medium sized law firm, with aspirations to increase turnover, profit, and PEP over the next three-year period. If the averages in the UK market are representative, our managing partner is probably male, in his mid-40s, and has been with the firm for around 11 years before making the step up to managing partner.

While relatively new in the post, he is determined to make his mark by delivering real change. In developing the firm's new strategy, he has consulted with the partnership and other key stakeholders across the firm. As you might expect, he has a range of views and opinions to take on board – many of which are conflicting. He, of course, has his personal views on which is the right path to take, and again these differ from many of the views from within the partnership.

He has also done his homework and read a wealth of information on the state of the legal market, forecast changes in buyer behavior, and the impact of new business structures. In fact, he is one report short of information overload.

So how does he decide which is the right route to take? What should be the cornerstone of the new strategy? Which approach will truly resonate with the market and therefore deliver the desired increased turnover, profits, and PEP?

What he really needs is a guide: someone on the inside.

The problem

This problem is not unique. All firms, of all shapes and sizes around the world, have the same issues that face our managing partner in developing, refining, and rolling out a strategy to the market. In fact, leaders of all businesses, regardless of their sector, have the same challenge – how do you identify the route that will deliver the best results?

The partnership structure, however, does bring with it its own unique set of challenges. With so many different personal views in the mix, managing expectations (and egos) can be difficult – not least when many of the consulted partners will have been in the firm for many, many years and will have a clear and often rather loud opinion on what works, and what does not.

There is also a strong temptation to look to other firms, to read up on their strategies and goals, and assume that if they are seeing success from their chosen route then their success can be replicated by simply following the same approach.

Ultimately, with so much information to take on board, many firms end up basing their strategy on a combination of previous internal experiences and the gut instinct of the leadership team.

This approach is prevalent across the professional services sector. On many occasions growth strategies are based purely on the recruitment of additional fee-earners. On paper this simple strategy will deliver the required results; after all, any new fee earner will translate to hundreds of hours of billable work per year, right?

There is an 'easy' potential path here for our managing partner. Yet basing growth strategies on simple mathematics and instinct also has its drawbacks.

Instinct is a dangerous thing

We all use and rely on instinct each and every day, and it certainly has its place. However, neither instinct nor intuition should form the basis of any business strategy. Why would we choose to rely on these intangible feelings and opinions when they can easily be tested? Without validation, our instincts are worth little more than good old fashioned hope.

For example, what happens when there is no work for the newly recruited fee earners, because the anticipated growth in your chosen sectors simply failed to materialize? What if your clients don't really "get" the new values you have pushed out to the market? What if differentiating yourself on your expertise isn't something your clients really respond to? What will the resultant struggling strategy do to the credibility of our fresh-faced managing partner?

All these things – and much, much more – can be tested and validated (or not, as the case may be) by simply consulting the guide.

The guide

Let your clients be your guide

Who knows better what clients want, and need, than the clients themselves?[1] Yet across the professional services sector, client listening is not nearly as well utilized as it should be. In other sectors (consumer goods, for example) asking clients about their needs, wants, and feedback on their purchases is now part of everyday life. Everything from buying a car to ordering dog food can trigger a feedback request.

Consumer brands collectively spend billions every year on understanding their market. They test new products and services before, during, and after launch. They use research to inform product refinements, their go-to-market strategy, and much more. And, while they have the mega-budgets available to do this sort of exercise, let's be frank – they only make that significant investment because they see the return. And then some.

Yet legal industry research suggests that only one in 10 law firm clients is asked for feedback. Why are firms so reluctant to embrace the very thing that will guide them to strategic success? Those that do invest in client listening are privy to a wealth of benefits.

More than just feedback

A number of firms conduct client feedback of some sort; however, in order to really extract maximum benefit from the exercise, firms need to ensure they ask all of the relevant questions, maximizing the time available, and really leverage the results across all aspects of the firm. Table 1 details just some of the things that can be achieved when you use your clients as a guide.

Remove risk and unnecessary spend	Get the best from your people
• Invest in a strategy that matches clients' needs and removes the risk of failure; • Only allocate budget (recruitment, marketing, or other) to areas of identified client need; and • Only undertake marketing activity that resonates with the market.	• Understand where team strengths and weaknesses lie; • Invest in training/shared learning where required; • Share feedback internally to improve morale and energy; and • Use client feedback within the appraisal process.
New client acquisition	**Client retention and growth**
• Base marketing and targeting on real strengths as identified by your clients; • Use identified "promoters" within the client base to leverage new relationships; • Use feedback within pitches and tenders to demonstrate excellence and case studies; and • Understand who the competitors really are, and differentiate accordingly.	• Identify issues with service delivery, expertise, or individuals before they arise; • Identify new revenue opportunities; • Demonstrate your commitment to your clients by engaging, listening, and actioning their feedback; • Increase loyalty by building deeper, more trusted relationships; and • Broaden relationships within your clients' (or your own) businesses.

Table 1: Realizing the benefits of using your clients as a guide

This matrix is not exhaustive. There are many other benefits and uses of client insights for those that take the time to collect, interpret, and use them. With all of this data to hand, strategy development suddenly becomes a straightforward – almost simple – process. And, what's more, it will work.

Basing your actions on what the market has told you it needs, and wants, means you have the best possible chance of success. To collect this sort of insight takes time and thought. You need a plan.

The plan

A client listening plan doesn't need to be overwhelmingly complex. It should, however, always have three core elements:

1. What do you want to achieve from the process?
2. Who are you going to speak to?
3. How are you going to collect the data?

What do you want to achieve?

This is the most important phase of any client listening program. Knowing what you want to achieve will help you to ensure you ask the right people the right questions, in the right way. Simply stating, "We want to get some feedback on our work" isn't going to deliver the insights you need to inform or transform your strategy.

The range of question areas is potentially limitless. However, there are some core areas that all firms should consider. These are outlined in Figure 1. Understanding which of these you wish to test, and their relative importance to you and your firm, will help you to structure your program in a way that will deliver meaningful – and, more importantly, actionable – results.

A number of these areas are more suited to qualitative research – that is to say, deeper conversations with a handful of key individuals – than quantitative research, which focuses on a more structured approach with a larger number of clients. The

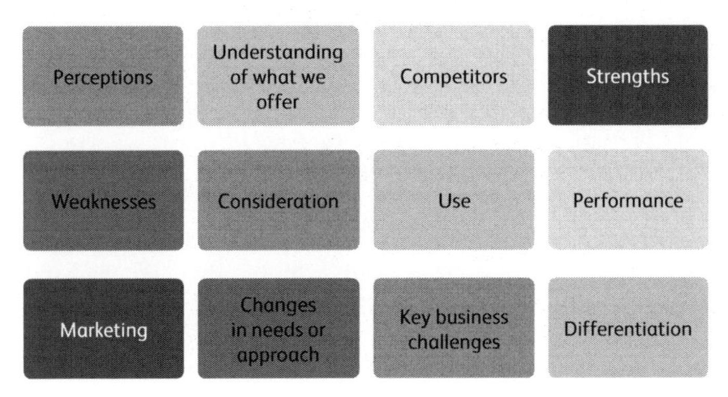

Figure 1: Core question areas to consider in your client listening program

benefits of each approach, and differences between the two, are outlined in Table 3.

Metrics that matter

If your firm already has a set of performance metrics in place that relate to your client facing strategy, then this is an ideal time to take a measure of performance. Alternatively, this is a great time to uncover what metrics are really relevant to you and your clients, and create your own set of bespoke benchmarks for measuring progress in the years to come. You may wish to consider, for example:

- Percentage of satisfied clients;
- Percentage of clients willing to recommend your services;
- Consideration levels for specific work types or in certain market segments;
- Existing market share in specific market segments or work types; and
- Effectiveness or relevance of your marketing activities.

Who are you going to speak to?

"Who?" is always a tricky question. Many firms only engage with their existing client base when it comes to client listening, and there are many good reasons to do so. However, by limiting your insights to those that already know and work with the firm, you risk missing out on some of the most valuable of insights available. These come from those that do not yet work with you. To be fully comprehensive, any client listening program should include existing clients, target clients, lost clients, referrers, and any other third party stakeholders that may instruct or refer work to your firm.

When it comes to existing clients, the next questions are typically "Which ones?" and "How many?"

Which ones?

Again, the answer to these questions should come from a clear understanding of what you are trying to achieve. Table 2 outlines just some of the benefits of engaging with different types of clients.

How many?

This is a very difficult question and is dependent on a number of factors, again relating closely to what it is you want to achieve. Budget is also a key consideration. That being said, extensive insights can be revealed through as little as half a dozen in-depth interviews with key clients. If just one relationship can be developed, cross-sold, or indeed saved, it is an investment well worth making.

Unlike typical market research, the aim is not only to understand what the "average" client thinks, but also to understand the nuances of each and every valuable client relationship – in an ideal world we would speak to each and every one. What we need, however, is an approach that allows us to engage with as many clients as possible within the budget, while providing robust feedback across the client landscape. Avoiding "cherry picking" your best clients is of course a good place to start.

Key clients	Understand how effective your relationship really is, where the value lies, and the potential for future work (including cross-selling). This is also a great opportunity to ensure key clients are aligned to the firm as well as to specific individuals.
Growth potential	These may be the key clients of the future, or perhaps are small income generators, but are potential brand ambassadors for your firm. Understanding your strengths and weaknesses relative to your competitors will help you ensure continued growth from this group of valuable clients.
Declining clients	An analysis of fee income over three to five years may reveal some interesting results. Knowing which clients have been declining spend over the period, and why, may provide an opportunity to revive the relationship before it is lost entirely.
Lost clients	Where clients have been lost to a competitor, whether via a formal procurement process or not, this is an ideal time to understand what the key factors were and apply that learning to future processes.
All other clients	In most firms, there is a mass of clients that do not fall into the above categories, but should not be ignored. This group is ideal for exploring service performance, satisfaction, and recommendation as well as understanding how they differentiate your firm against the competition.

Table 2: The benefits of engagement with different client types

When it comes to specific numbers, conventional methodologies suggest that a minimum sample size of 30 should be used to reduce the risk of error, and this is certainly a good starting point. However, the "right" number of respondents varies in every situation depending on things like the overall size of the population at hand, the amount of possible error you can tolerate in your overall results, and whether or not you want to be able to break down your results by client type, service type, office location, and so on.

Statistical error might be of absolutely no consequence to your firm if you are taking a purely qualitative approach to the interviews – but it might be very important if you want to publish results claiming that "X percent of our clients are highly satisfied with our service." Likewise, if you're offering anonymity to your client respondents, you need to include sufficient people to ensure they are not identifiable as part of a small group. For example, breaking down your results by office location might yield only one or two respondents for a particular office, meaning that it would be relatively easy to identify "anonymous" feedback.

Some firms opt for a smaller number of interviews with an emphasis on understanding their key clients and developing those relationships as a key focus of the program. As detailed above, while this approach has its uses, you do need to be aware that you might be missing highly valuable information from those second or third tier clients who, with a slightly different approach, might actually become key clients.

There are no hard and fast rules to dictate the number of interviews that should be conducted, so take your time over this phase of the process. Depending on your specific requirements, it is worth seeking advice from a research specialist to understand how many interviews should be sought, and with whom.

How are you going to collect the data?

Now we know what we are trying to achieve and with whom, we are ready to explore the right methodologies for your firm and your clients. Research methodologies fall into one of two categories: qualitative or quantitative (see Table 3 for a description of each).

Qualitative
These are in-depth interviews, typically conducted face to face or by telephone. They follow a question "guide" rather than a formally structured questionnaire, which allows the client to talk around areas that are of most interest and importance to them. They provide a richness and depth of insight not found in the quantitative stage. These are ideal for key clients and provide real value back to the commissioning firm. Typically, outputs from this process include detailed, written reports from each completed interview. These are ideal for informing key client teams, partners, or even sector groups. Often insights from these interviews deliver new revenue opportunities.
Quantitative
These are more structured interviews, which can be undertaken by phone or by web survey. They usually contain a large proportion of closed or scored questions, with only a few open ended questions. These are ideal for testing findings found in the qualitative phase or measuring specific areas such as performance, satisfaction, or value. The more structured approach means this methodology is ideal for ongoing measurement against key metrics. Results can often be segmented by client type, sector, practice area, or geography to reveal strengths and relative weaknesses across the firm.

Table 3: Qualitative and quantitative methodologies

In an ideal world, firms would always undertake a mixture of the two approaches in order to provide a fully rounded and statistically validated view from their clients and markets. That said, never underestimate the immense value that a single interview can provide.

The results

Data without action is pointless. Having invested the time, energy and budget in understanding the views and needs of your clients and the wider target market, you need to make that investment work as hard as possible.

Here are the top 10 ways to utilize the data collected, which in turn will guide you to success:

1. Validate (or re-write) your strategy;
2. Align recruitment, business development, and marketing spend with areas of anticipated growth;
3. Align your marketing and recruitment messages with what clients (and the market) say differentiates you;
4. Align training and personal development programs with the needs identified;
5. Develop relevant key metrics (and measure them!);
6. Feed data into sector and practice working groups;
7. Feed data into key account programs;
8. Share results with the entire firm – highlight strengths, weaknesses, and plans for improvement. Also report progress regularly;
9. Utilize verbatim comments in your marketing materials, pitches, tender documents, and directory/award submissions; and
10. Share a summary of the results with your clients, thank them for their contribution to your strategy, and highlight any developments you plan to make as a result.

Using your clients as your guide to your strategy simply removes the risk from the process. This authenticity in approach will truly set you apart.

It remains to be seen which route the managing partners of tomorrow will take. But as the legal sector further embraces approaches seen in the wider business and consumer sectors, the client view is likely to increase exponentially in importance.

Reference

1. "Client" refers to both existing and target clients, as well as any other parties that may refer or instruct work.

Chapter 4:
Crafting a cross-selling culture shift – An eight-phased approach

By David H. Freeman, JD, CEO of the David Freeman Consulting Group

As a law firm leader, you are regularly consumed with finding ways to get your lawyers to pursue their best business development opportunities, with the best of the best often found through cross-selling. Getting your lawyers to share your level of passion, however, is another story altogether.

For many lawyers, the concept of cross-selling evokes a negative reaction. The reasons vary – for some, they fear the client will only see it as a desperate, firm-centered attempt to make more money. Others remember bad experiences in their past, where the lawyer who was cross-sold did not perform well, resulting in serious damage to the client relationship. And yet others may see no financial incentive, and possibly a disincentive, in making cross-introductions.

To successfully initiate a robust cross-selling effort requires thoughtful planning and firm-wide commitment. In the following sections I will suggest a structure to help you identify your firm's particular challenges, build approaches to address those challenges, and develop disciplines for embedding the proper behaviors into the cultural fabric of your firm.

Change the game

A good place to start is inside the heads of your lawyers. If you positively reframe how they perceive cross-selling, you're likely to get more of their time and energy devoted to it. This can begin with a simple, but powerful, change in language. I suggest eliminating the phrase "cross-selling" from your firm's vocabulary, and replacing it with "cross-serving". Removing "selling" from the equation reduces some of negative impressions conjured up by that word, whereas "serving" denotes actions that live on higher moral ground.

Making service a bedrock value can also act like a cultural glue to further unite the firm. A deep commitment to service can get lawyers working together for the common good, create stronger interpersonal connections and trust, make partners and associates less inclined to leave, and send positive signals to laterals that your firm is a great platform for growing a practice.

Cross-serving as a catalyst for change

Many firms get stuck when trying to figure out how to invigorate their overall culture of business development. The beauty of concentrating on cross-serving is the cascade of positive benefits that can flow from this initiative. Cross-serving often delivers swift financial returns, which means firm members will quickly see fruits from their labor. This kind of success breeds additional success, so more lawyers should jump on the bandwagon once they see what the earlier adopters have accomplished. It also can serve as a trigger to set many other desirable actions in motion. Firms that are fully committed to a cross-serving culture shift would likely:

- Ask for more client feedback;
- Build higher performing client and industry teams;
- Deliver enhanced levels of client service;
- Know, like, and trust each other better;
- Work more effectively across offices and practices;
- Develop the right measures to track progress and eventual success;
- Develop leaders who effectively manage business development; and
- Not allow slippage back to old patterns of behavior.

The eight phases of a cross-serving culture shift

If there is anything you've learned in your role as a law firm leader, it's that significant change does not happen on its own. To help you effectively manage this process, the following eight-phased approach can be used to inculcate new habits into your organization.

1. Make the big decisions

There is a huge difference between "We *should* do more cross-serving", and "We *will* do more cross-serving". Firms need an unwavering commitment from senior leaders in order to withstand the inevitable fits and starts associated with a potentially disruptive culture change. Set your stake firmly in the ground by gaining their consensus on the importance of cross-serving, and eliciting their whole-hearted pledge to do what it takes to make it a reality. To help get your leaders to this stage you can ask them questions like:

- "Are we happy with the way the firm is performing?"
- "If we're not happy with our performance, is it important for us to make changes?"
- "If it is important for us to make changes, what must change?"
- "After analyzing the benefits of cross-serving, is this a change we need to make?" And
- "What commitments must we make as a leadership team to "guarantee" we will become better at cross-serving?"

2. Identify obstacles

In the past you've probably tried to get more cross-serving activity to occur, only to be disappointed by the results. Successful implementation requires a clear-eyed look at what gets in the way of realizing your cross-serving potential. As an exercise, work with your leaders to identify the major obstacles that impede your progress. The following are examples of some of the common issues you might be facing:

- Poor internal coordination/communication of opportun--ities;
- Internal politics/silos;
- Inadequate internal relationship-building and trust;
- Leaders who don't adequately manage cross-serving efforts;
- Poor communication of cross-services to existing clients;
- Misaligned compensation systems; and
- Relationship lawyers who are reluctant to make an introduction.

3. Increase lawyer engagement

Before the plan can be implemented, you need people who care enough to dedicate the necessary energy to make it successful. As you've experienced, you're in a constant battle for your lawyers' time and attention, so you must find ways to make their priorities align with yours.

The following are several approaches for increasing their engagement to fire up the engines of change:

- Build the business case for why this initiative makes so much sense, especially how it serves the best interests of their clients, makes for a stronger firm, protects client relationships, and increases compensation;
- Engage people in collaborative planning so *they* understand what needs to be done, and *they* roll up their sleeves to craft solutions. This approach tends to create a greater sense of personal ownership, which should in turn increase their desire to see *their* plan succeed;
- Find the coalition of the willing who will do what it takes to make the magic happen. This front-end-of-the-bell-curve

group can offer the proof others need to show it's well worth the effort;

- Put like-minded, high passion people together to hunt as a pack. Good teams can get more done, create better decisions, and increase accountability; and
- Make it extremely clear that the firm values these activities by rewarding and recognizing those who act in alignment with the cross-serving plan.

4. Create a plan

Along with leaders who are fully on board, the identification of major obstacles, and approaches for getting more from your lawyers, you must also build a solid plan of attack. During this phase you dissect the process to uncover your strengths and weaknesses, prioritize where to focus your firm's attention, determine the timing and sequence of implementation, and develop specific action steps and measures. In phase six of this process, I will suggest several key initiatives that can jumpstart the success of your cross-serving efforts.

5. Remove or reduce obstacles

It is one thing to identify what gets in the way of your success, and quite another to do something about it. In conjunction with phase three (the planning process), take a good look at the major obstacles you identified and come up with ways to tear down those walls. You will find that many of the Key Accelerators presented in the next section can serve to both reduce your barriers and facilitate faster growth.

6. Activate the Accelerators

This brings us to the crescendo of the eight-phased process. You know you can't tackle all things at the same time, so think of implementation as a cascade. Just as in bowling, where you must hit a pin in just the right way to knock down the others, here, too, you must pick the right initiatives to "hit" first, to trigger other desired actions.

In the box-out I suggest 13 "Key Accelerators" of cross-serving. As a savvy leader, you can strategically choose one or two that can both directly improve your performance and get the ball rolling in other areas. One example of how to activate this domino effect is by starting with the Client Feedback Accelerator:

- Deeply listening to clients often uncovers the need to deliver higher levels of service (Client Service Accelerator);
- Improved levels of service, especially with larger clients, may manifest in higher performing teams (Client/Industry Team Accelerator); and
- To maximize effectiveness both before and after receiving feedback, lawyers may need to learn more about each other to develop a better understanding of additional services they can offer to their clients (Internal Cross-Connections Accelerator, Internal Giving Accelerator, and Internal Approach Accelerator).

13 Key Accelerators of cross-serving

- The Client Feedback Accelerator;
- The Key Client and Industry Team Accelerator;
- The Exceptional Client Service Accelerator;
- The Internal Cross-Connections Accelerator;
- The Internal Giving Accelerator;
- The Internal Approach Accelerator;
- The Client Contact Accelerator;
- The Technology Accelerator;
- The Compensation Accelerator;
- The Key Measures Accelerator;

- The Internal Communication/PR/Education Accelerator;
- The Accountability Accelerator; and
- The Leadership Mega-Accelerator.

7. Develop the right measures

I've specifically highlighted this Key Accelerator because of its subtle yet powerful importance.

While we typically watch the end-of-the-day numbers – more revenue in different practice areas from existing clients – you must keep a careful eye on the up-front behaviors that go into delivering those final results.

To track your progress in creating a healthy cross-serving culture, you can measure activity in your highest priority Key Accelerators. Examples might include:

- Client feedback meetings conducted;
- Meetings between cross-practice group leaders to discuss cross-opportunities;
- Internal presentations made cross-groups to learn about other practices; and
- Introductions to clients made by the relationship lawyer to new lawyers in the firm.

8. Prevent slippage

As stated earlier, real change will not happen on its own. To keep from being disappointed, and to minimize wasted time and energy, I suggest making the following sweeping assumption: people will not follow through on their commitments to change unless they are actively managed to do so. In the book *Make it Stick*[1] the authors share a powerful observation: it is part of human nature to forget! Making things stick requires you to interrupt the natural process of forgetting, and implement systems to keep people from sliding back into old, less productive patterns of behavior.

This phase is where the lockdown occurs. To keep your well-intentioned initiatives from fading away due to a lack of commitment and follow-through, you must find ways to keep your proverbial foot on the gas. This requires people to step up to champion the process, and there is no one with greater power and authority than you, the managing partner.

As the person sitting in the buck-stops-here chair, the managing partner must play the role of chief implementation officer, acting as a "watcher" who holds people accountable to deliver on their commitments. You must handle the inevitable pushback – the active and passive resistance to new initiatives – and act as overlords to hold firm to the vision and prevent slippage back to less effective ways of doing things. Some effective "watching" approaches include:

- Provide ongoing reminders to refresh recollection of key elements of the plan;
- Conduct regular training to improve effectiveness;
- Conduct internal PR to praise desired behavior;
- Assign "deputies" such as group or team leaders to implement sub-elements of the plan;
- Measure individual progress, and make those measures transparent;
- Develop a sense of urgency; and
- Tie progress and success to compensation.

Creating a culture of cross-serving takes significant vision, courage, finesse, street-smarts, and stamina. It requires you, as managing partner, to communicate and evangelize more than you ever thought necessary. By developing a well-conceived plan, reducing obstacles, pushing the right organizational buttons, and not allowing people to fall back into lower performance habits, you can leapfrog past your competitors and reap substantial rewards.

Reference

1. Brown, P., Roediger, H. and McDaniel, M., *Make It Stick: The Science of Successful Learning*, Massachusetts: Harvard University Press, 2014.

Chapter 5: **Lateral hiring can be key to client growth – If you do it right**

By Ian Turvill, chief marketing officer at Freeborn & Peters LLP

Too many firms bring in new partners with expectations of significant client growth, but ultimately fail to realize the anticipated gains. Firms that develop new and/or expanded client relationships as a result of their lateral hiring recognize three critical success factors:

- First, they develop a strategy and a plan for lateral hiring as a whole, and then in regard to each and every new attorney they bring onboard;
- Second, they recognize that profitable lateral integration starts way before a candidate receives an offer, and it extends far past the hire date; and
- Third, they apply close scrutiny to performance versus plan and make appropriate course corrections.

This chapter explains each of these concepts in turn, providing a constructive and systematic means to assure client growth through their lateral hiring practices.

Critical success factor 1 – Develop and communicate an explicit strategy for lateral hires

As the senior marketer at a mid-sized firm, I spend a lot of time coaching attorneys. To simplify my message, and to provide a framework for our discussions, I use an acronym based on four words – "Goals", "Relationships", "Originations", and "Work" – that is, GROW. There is great power in this simple, strategic approach, because attorneys quickly understand and appreciate how the four component parts must be developed and then applied in concert.

"GROW" can also help firm leaders plan the activities necessary to make lateral hiring a success. In this context, GROW means:

- **Goals** – Understand and describe explicitly how a lateral hire contributes to the implementation of the firm's strategy;
- **Relationships** – Exploit the relationships that the lateral hire brings to the firm and vice versa;
- **Originations** – Support the hire's every effort in winning new business; and
- **Work** – Monitor and measure the quality of the lateral hire's work to ensure the firm's reputation is enhanced, and not harmed.

The many activities underlying these four components are best understood in the context of the second critical success factor.

Critical success factor 2 – Recognize that successful integration begins long before and extends far after the hire date

Successful lateral integration that contributes significantly to client growth should involve five key phases:

- **Phase 1: Targeting and filtering** – Scanning for high-potential lateral hire candidates;
- **Phase 2: Recruiting and attracting** – Assessing fit and performance of possible new hires;
- **Phase 3: Onboarding** – Helping a lateral hire quickly become an effective contributor;

- **Phase 4: Planning and execution** – Developing and implementing a plan that drives success; and
- **Phase 5: Tracking and accountability** – Measuring progress against the plan and applying incentives to maximize performance.

An appropriate way to understand these phases better is to apply the questions suggested by the components of GROW, as shown in Table 1.

The descriptions below "peel the onion" for each of the first four phases. The last phase of "Tracking and accountability" represents something that differentiates successful firms to such a degree that it is a critical success factor unto itself.

Phase 1 – Targeting and filtering

What are the specific goals of the firm, and how will they be addressed through a lateral hire?

Firms can either respond to a headhunter's proposals, or they can search deliberately for the best candidates. In general, firms should place greater weight on the latter approach.

Even if a firm does rely on headhunters as a source of candidates, if it has not clearly defined its goal then it can never hope to screen candidates effectively. Goals should include answers to: "What clients are we targeting?"; "What services will we be promoting?"; "How will we differentiate ourselves from other firms?"; and "What sales growth are we expecting?"

Among the clients/segments/practice areas we are targeting, which attorneys from other firms know key decision makers?

Equipped with these goals, a firm can explore at least three different routes to identify possible lateral hires for it to approach:

- Consult clients or prospects in targeted segments and simply ask them who they rely upon for legal services;

	Phase I: Targeting and filtering	Phase II: Recruiting and attracting
	Pre-hire: Questions to answer	
Goals	• What are the specific goals of the firm, and how will they be addressed through the lateral hire?	• Does a prospective candidate have a clear set of career objectives, and do they align with the firm's goals?
Relationships	• Among the clients/ segments/practice areas we are targeting, which partners from other firms know key decision makers?	• Is there proof positive that the candidate has established relationships and an appropriate reputation within the target market?
Originations	• What are the primary marketing and business development techniques used by our firm? • Are they consistent with the practices seen among our target clients?	• Does the candidate's professed and demonstrated approach to business development match the firm's approach and its available resources?
Work	• What capabilities and experiences are necessary to serve the clients we are targeting? • What are the service expectations of the clients we serve and/or wish to serve?	• Does the candidate possess the desired capabilities and experience? • Are there clear indicators that the candidate delivers a superior level of service?

Table 1 – The elements of GROW applied to the five phases of successful lateral integration[1]

Phase III: Onboarding	Phase IV: Planning and execution	Phase V: Tracking and accountability
	Post-hire: Steps to take	
• Share all documents describing the firm's strategy	• Engage in a joint planning exercise among the hire, practice group leaders, and firm leadership to establish specific goals for client growth	• Document client-related activity and results • Assess performance relative to potential and established goals • Apply remedial action when progress falls short, and take advantage if it is exceeding expectations
• Import the hire's contacts from all available sources, including Outlook, LinkedIn, CRM systems, business cards, etc. • Cross-reference the hire's and the firm's contacts and determine how they complement each other	• Establish specific targets for client growth: – Where can the new hire share the capabilities of their new firm to expand their existing client relationships? – Where can the firm share the newly acquired capabilities to expand its existing client relationships? – What new relationships may be possible as a result of the combination of the firm and the new hire together?	• Establish if the relationships as presented and discussed in Phases II and IV have panned out
• Communicate the hire's arrival and maximize the proportion of client transfers • Inventory representative matters where the lateral hire played a leading role, even if completed at prior firms • Make them available across all marketing channels		• Determine the business development role of the hire going forward: – Can they share skills through mentoring? – Do they need coaching or support to realize their potential?
• Ensure the hire is properly coached in all relevant administrative systems, e.g. timekeeping, document management, etc.	• Establish how the new hire will be supported by firm resources (associates, technology, etc.) to maximize the quality of service • Determine the nature and level of support to be provided by marketing and business development	• Measure the quality of work and client service through interviews with internal and external sources

- Use online sources such as Thomson Reuters Monitor Suite to identify attorneys who are "rising stars" in areas of interest; and
- Search for articles and commentaries in areas of interest and find the leading attorneys in targeted domains.

What are the primary marketing and business development techniques used by our firm? And are they consistent with the practices seen among our target clients?
Some firms may favor advertising or sponsorship as a way of gaining attention; others may build new client relationships through direct outreach and a "personal touch". Firms will be best served when they understand their practices and assess whether a lateral candidate fits their model. It is also important to consider whether target clients in this domain prefer one style of business development over another and ask whether the firm is equipped to support that.

What capabilities and experiences are necessary to serve the clients we are targeting?
A firm can address this question in several ways:

- Review the types of litigation that targeted clients are currently facing;
- Examine or simply reflect on the most likely legal issues targets must address; and
- Ask whether there are legal concerns that are unique to the target market – often these are of a regulatory nature.

What are the service expectations of the clients we serve and/or wish to serve?
Akin to the issue of preferred business development methods, it is vitally important to understand clients' expectations of service in the segments that the firm currently serves or that it wishes to serve.

Phase 2 – Recruiting and attracting

Does a prospective candidate have a clear set of career objectives, and do they align with the firm's goals?

An attorney who has a written business development plan will have a far greater likelihood of success than someone who flies by the seat of their pants. A documented approach to business development is so critical to success that any candidate who does not have a plan – or who refuses to develop one on request – should be discarded.

Is there proof positive that the candidate has established relationships and an appropriate reputation within the target market?

The question of reputation is relatively easy to dispatch, particularly if the firm has sought out a candidate based on the brand they may have established through writing and speaking. Also, while lawyer ranking services have limitations, those that are based on actual client feedback such as *Chambers* should be given far greater weight.

Relationships are much harder to assess. Some degree of skepticism is appropriate – "Do they truly know and have influence with the senior legal officers at the corporations they reference? Or are they simply part of a much larger team and have collected a few business cards along the way?"

Does the candidate's professed and demonstrated approach to business development match the firm's approach and its available resources?

Different firms have a different philosophy of client development. Some may place an emphasis on pursuits based around teams of attorneys, while others may rely on "lone wolf" rainmakers. Consider, too, a situation where a partner comes from a much larger firm to a much smaller one where there are far fewer marketing and business development resources.

Phase 3 – Onboarding

Share all documents describing the firm's strategy

If the firm has been holding back in any way, then now is the time to share as much information as possible about goals and strategies and to make background information such as market research or client feedback studies available to the new hire. The new partner should be encouraged to read and reflect on the information that is shared.

Import the hire's contacts from all available sources, including Outlook, LinkedIn, CRM systems, business cards, etc.

It is critical that the new hire is mandated to fulfill this task, even if they have to rely on significant clerical assistance to get it done. These contacts are one of the raw materials from which the lateral hire's value will be fully realized.

Cross-reference the hire's candidates with the firm's contacts and determine how they complement each other

There are at least three perspectives that should be applied, and these are discussed in greater depth in the "Planning and execution" phase. At this point in the integration process, it should be incumbent on the marketing/business development department to examine the data and develop initial hypotheses about where the greatest areas of opportunity lie.

Communicate the hire's arrival and maximize the proportion of client transfers

Any clients where the lateral hire is playing an active part of a matter should be the first to be transferred. In addition, all former client contacts should receive a communication indicating that the partner has switched firms – a "celebratory" postcard will often suffice.

The lateral partner should also prioritize other clients who have not been active recently, but which:

- Have the greatest likelihood of yielding future work; and
- Are likely to be targets of the firm the partner left.

During the "Planning and execution" phase, these should be the focus of targeted outreach.

Inventory representative matters where the lateral hire played a leading role – even if completed at prior firms

The new hire brings new experience and capabilities to the firm, allowing it to pitch new services to existing clients and to prospects. However, the firm will not be aware of them unless they are properly documented and cataloged.

Make them available across all marketing channels

It is vital that the new firm brings to bear the new credentials gathered from the lateral partner by ensuring that they are presented not only as part of their biography, but also as part of any relevant firm marketing materials, especially pitches or proposals.

Ensure the hire is properly coached in all relevant administrative systems, e.g. timekeeping, document management, interactions with paralegals, staffing by associates, etc.

A firm will lose valuable productivity and engagement if it doesn't consider consciously the "systems" – broadly defined – that the new partner will be called upon to use. These include the specific computer systems and applications that will support them day to day, but also whatever formal processes may exist to request the support of paralegals, associates, and other human resources.

Phase 4 – Planning and execution

Engage in a joint planning exercise among the hire, practice group leaders, and firm leadership to establish specific goals for client growth

Once a lateral partner is free from the distractions of onboarding, and also liberated from any limitations on the open exchange of information, they should sit and plan with the leaders of their practice group; if the hire is critical enough, then firm leadership may also get involved.

There are several basic questions that must be answered over the course of one or more sessions:

- What are the specific practice areas where the attorney is going to have the greatest focus?
- What specific clients or types of clients will they be targeting?
- What are the specific marketing activities that they will fulfill? And
- What business development goals will be realized by the new partner, and by when?

A partner may be reluctant to commit to a goal, because they know they will be held to account – but that's the point! To overcome the natural resistance to goal-setting, a firm should put in place a minimum acceptable goal, a goal that reflects a reasonable expectation of success, and a stretch goal.

The answers to these four questions should be informed in part by the outcomes of the analysis described in the next recommended step.

Establish specific targets for client growth

- Where can the new hire share the capabilities of their new firm to expand their existing client relationships?
- Where can the firm share the newly acquired capabilities to expand its existing client relationships? And
- What new relationships may be possible as a result of the combination of the firm and the new hire together?

When the firm's marketing department cross-referenced the lateral hire's contacts with those of the firm, it gained important insights into the potential to make beneficial introductions.

Too often, when a lateral hire joins a firm, the range of possible new connections is considered across just one dimension, and firms may fail to consider other permutations. Successful firms will consider all potential angles to ensure that the full value of additions to their ranks is realized.

Establish how the new hire will be supported by firm resources (associates, paralegals, technology, etc.) to maximize the quality of service

With so much responsibility placed primarily, though certainly not exclusively, on the shoulders of the new attorney, it is not only fair but also vital that they know they have the firm's support in very practical ways.

Determine the nature and level of support to be provided by marketing and business development

There is probably no area more important to define what support will be provided to the attorney than in the area of marketing and business development.

Critical success factor 3 – Apply close scrutiny to performance versus plan and make course corrections over time

In "Planning and execution", we indicated that firms establish *specific* goals for performance. It is in "Tracking and accountability" (Phase 5) that the firm should apply a timely and constructive regimen of measurement and subsequent rewards, penalties, and course corrections.

Document client-related activity and results

Successful firms do not wait to see if the new partner's efforts bear fruit. The partner should be documenting their business development activities – how much outreach have they undertaken through phone calls, email, or seminars? How many client visits have they made? How many pitches have they presented to prospective clients? If the new partner cannot demonstrate that they are completing the activities necessary to build business then this may be reason for concern.

Assess performance relative to established goals

Coupled with regular reports of activity, there should also be frequent (at least once per quarter) in person meetings to review performance. If the partner is falling short, then the purpose of such meetings is not necessarily to drag them over the coals. Instead, there should be a frank discussion of what's working and what's not, on all sides.

Apply remedial action when progress falls short, and take advantage if it is exceeding expectations

The great challenge exists in choosing an appropriate response to a partner's shortfall.

If a firm's response is too harsh, then the partner may be demotivated; they may even be tempted to jump ship. However, if a firm's response is too soft, then the partner may continue to bumble along without making much progress.

The key then is to have a range of responses that match the scale of the gap between expectations and reality. The path taken should be tuned to the firm's culture; to the leader's assessment of the circumstances; and to the firm's financial circumstances.

Responses may include:

- Pairing the partner with another member of the firm who can help them to stay accountable;
- Recalibrating the strategy to take into account lessons learned so far;
- Changing expectations of the partner's role, including placing greater emphasis on hours billed than on matters originated;
- Revising goals downward – and changing compensation to suit; and

- Indicating that the time has come to part ways, and providing some period over which the partner can seek new employment and depart gracefully.

Of course, there is a flipside to this – it is entirely conceivable that the partner is "hitting it out of the park" and handily beating the goals that have been set. In this case, the firm should take steps to give the partner more resources and to take fullest advantage of this potential goldmine.

Establish if the relationships as presented and discussed in phases 2 and 4 have panned out

One of the most important ways in which firms can assess a partner's progress and contribution is to review the development of the relationships outlined in phase 4. If these are moving forward, but they have not yet been as productive as hoped, then the new partner can be granted some leeway. If relationships are not developing, then the partner's potential to help the firm win new business may have been overstated and overestimated – and a harsher approach in terms of remedial action may be necessary.

Determine the business development role of the hire going forward

- Can they share skills through mentoring?
- Do they need coaching or support to realize their potential?

If the new partner is proving to be successful in their business development efforts, then their impact on the firm can be further magnified by having them serve as a mentor to others in the firm.

If it appears that they have the right attitude, and they are applying a significant effort, but they are still somehow coming up short, then it may be appropriate to engage a business development coach who can hone their skills.

Measure the quality of work and client service through interviews with internal and external sources

Firms that are successful in their lateral integration efforts will assess the new partner's work from the get-go. They will speak first with the attorneys with whom the lateral hire collaborates and then, as their body of work grows, with the clients for whom they are providing services.

Conclusion

Hiring new partners to a firm is an expensive and risky proposition. It is the responsibility of firm leadership to do all it can to maximize the return on its investment in new talent and to elevate the likelihood of success. Whether a firm follows the steps precisely as laid out here is unimportant. However, a structured approach with clear strategy and goals, an emphasis on planning, ongoing scrutiny over an extended period, and a willingness to make course corrections are essential elements without which firms will find lateral integration to be a salary sinkhole, rather than a source of enhanced value.

Reference

1. This table appeared previously on http://ProfessionalServices.guru Reproduced with permission.

Chapter 6: **Why creativity and innovation are the key to value enhancement for legal departments**

By Deepa Tharmaraj, legal director at Dell Middle East, Africa & Turkey

In this article I consider how in-house counsels' value enhancement strategies can positively influence the growth strategies of law firms, by providing insights into a legal department's innovative solutions and their drivers for creativity and innovation. I am speaking about creativity and innovation from a legal counsel's perspective – in an in-house legal department – but these principles can be applied to lawyers in general.[1]

Drivers of a changing market from the client's perspective

There are five things that every law firm needs to know about its clients; often clients tell the firm two or three of these things, but not all five. Understanding their clients' needs will reveal that general counsel in legal departments have the same pressures as their businesses do, and the same pressures as the law firms do: keeping the cost down and meeting the key performance indicators such as value-added services, operational excellence, and client satisfaction.

Law firms recognize that their clients, as buyers, are innovating to extract best value from their vendors and are testing out new procurement practices to identify new sources of service providers. The question is, what makes a law firm stand out in the eyes of this generation of legal service buyers? Do law firms understand that legal departments have to change and that, unless they change, they will not survive in their current shape? Naturally, these changes permeate through their relationships with outside counsel, and may shed light on why in-house counsel are demanding change from the law firms they appoint.

Law firms need to accept that they are pivotal to the success of the legal department and its business. Before exploring this, I want to share the five things that every law firm needs to know about the legal departments it works with:

1. Legal departments are prioritizing simplification, standardization, and automation of routine work and templates of contracts and letters;
2. Legal counsel invest time and effort in building long term and open relationships, based on trust, with their outside counsel;
3. In-house lawyer and outside counsel engagement increases where the parties are co-creating innovative solutions collaboratively, and sharing the pain and gain of these innovative solutions;
4. Legal counsel expect accurate and precise advice from their outside counsel – there is very little room for error or doubt; and
5. Legal counsel want to see their outside counsel driving value creation, and translating that to value-added services for the legal department as a natural by-product of the relationship.

With the democratization of legal services, legal counsel are increasingly relying on the existing tools and resources within their organization in order to innovate and are refusing to pay extra money for things that they can do themselves. However, it is fair to say that not all legal counsel apply innovative thinking. Could the resistance to innovate stem from our legal training?

In-house lawyers have multi-disciplinary stakeholders, and businesses' expectations of in-house legal departments are changing considerably. The business and its legal counsel are interdependent; however, that interdependency has to be balanced with the independence required of a legal counsel who has to prioritize the role of risk manager. Our job is to connect the business, support functions and operations, and to ensure compliance at all levels. Business needs and regulatory requirements are changing rapidly and therefore the speed at which we have to respond to those needs is increasing dramatically, primarily due to the technology that is available today. With these demands from the business and a regulated environment, both law firms and legal counsel need the agility and zeal of a start-up to develop innovative ideas which will enable and empower the general counsel to meet the legal department's KPIs.

I have divided this article loosely into three main themes:

1. Culture to innovate;
2. Opportunities to innovate; and
3. Tools for innovation.

There is a plethora of research and literature on the first two sections in legal publications, and materials on change management and culture, and those interested in reading further on this subject should look to the several esteemed publications and authors cited in this chapter. I will also discuss tools for innovation – because these are tools that are not specifically designed for legal practitioners. Years of working with researchers and engineers had aroused my curiosity to search for ways to innovate in my legal role, and I describe some of these in this article. As for the law firms, this article is an opportunity to see things from our perspective and how we are developing innovative ideas to meet our client needs and KPIs.

Creativity and innovation

> *"If we never do anything which has not been done before, we shall never get anywhere. The law will stand still while the rest of the world goes on, and that will be bad for both."*
> Lord Denning, *Packer v Packer* [1954]

Before I proceed, we need to be on the same page about the definitions of creativity and innovation. "Creativity is the capability or act of conceiving something original or unusual. Innovation is the implementation of something new"[2] because innovation is the ability to apply a new approach to a fundamental problem which could result in an incremental or a breakthrough benefit.

I think the rigorous law training during the undergraduate or pre-law program, and the subsequent Bar and law school, develops abstract thinking, problem solving, and analytical skills, especially through the countless hours of cramming case law and codified statutes – and not to mention all the Latin words! I am convinced that the demanding law training has prepared us for the highest order of thinking skills. Bloom's Taxonomy was developed by Benjamin Bloom to set out six classifications of thinking corresponding to cognitive levels of complexity.[3] The six classifications are remembering, understanding, applying, analyzing, evaluation, and creation. Creation! Since creation involves something new and possibly useful, I believe that our legal training has equipped us to be creative and innovative; but we often stop before we embark on the next step. The central tenet of this article is to highlight the importance of embracing the culture of innovation in legal departments, and look at examples of the types of opportunities that are available to legal counsel working in small or large in-house legal departments, whether in headquarters or regional offices.

Culture to innovate

> *"To truly experience living and not merely existing throughout our (legal) careers, business and life, the progressive evolutionary dynamics of our present decade (and beyond for that matter) is compelling us to get out of our comfort zones, to dare to be different, and ultimately to re-invent ourselves."* Chrissie Lightfoot, *Tomorrow's Naked Lawyer*

Many legal departments today are experimenting with new business models, process improvements, and technology-led systems and tools to extract value and cost savings in response to the incredible pressures they are facing from their cost centers. The challenges and the problems we face could be bucketized roughly into the triangle of people, process, and technology. We could connect innovative ideas to one of the three pillars, which represent a rudimentary framework for the purposes of this article, and each pillar if explored in conjunction with the tools of innovation could produce some powerful and innovative results.

People

Innovation starts with an individual who has an idea, and the motivation to develop the idea to solve a problem. But the motivation has to drive the initiative to obtain stakeholders' buy-in, build a prototype of the idea, test the idea, implement change management, and finally share the end product with other team members. This may work in an ideal world, but the challenge is that every one of the described steps involves the availability of time and collaboration with colleagues and peers on the part of the individual lawyer. In reality, turning a kernel of an idea into full-blown innovation and solution is a monumental quest. So the question we always ask is: why does one company's in-house department get its act together and produce innovative results in a sustainable manner, while another company of a comparable status does not? Does the answer lie with the leadership?

A leader in an in-house legal department, who promotes and encourages original ideas and process improvements and embraces technology to modernize the legal department and its people, will make innovation happen. A leader who engages their people to think innovatively and work collaboratively across teams, lines of business, and support functions (e.g. finance, tax, and HR) will foster innovation. A step further: successful innovative environments accept failure as an essential ingredient to innovation. Failures or mistakes do not have to be celebrated, but should be investigated to explore the reason for the unsuccessful innovation. When we collaborate, we bring different perspectives and flavors of interpretation to the problem. Unless the different perspectives are managed in a cohesive manner in a team environment, the ideas and perspectives could create awkwardness or a hostile environment. In *Collective Genius*,[4] the concept of "creative abrasion" has been used to reinforce the theory that innovative solutions emerge from "a series of sparks, not from a single flash of insight, as group members play off one another, each member's contribution inspiring the next." So constructive feedback and powerful criticism, when applied properly, can be "an engine of innovation".[5] Vineet Nayar of HCL Technologies said in *Collective Genius* that innovative leaders are "social architects"; collective result outstrips individual effort when the team is led by a leader who prioritizes innovation in every aspect – time, resources, and money.

Process

The one constant that charts across every part of an organization is process. An end-to-end process in a framework aims to capture a holistic view of internal control systems to manage, produce, or deliver something. It delineates dependencies and inter-dependencies between lines of business or functions; if the process is robust and is complied with, we grow in efficiency and competitiveness. Process can also stifle innovation if it is applied and approached in a rigid manner. But with the innovation trend bucking up, we are starting to recognize process innovation resulting in process improvements. Replacing a manual process for work intake and allocation to a team of lawyers with an automated system of self-triage questions and answers, culminating with a web-based intake process, is an innovation that in-house legal departments have deployed successfully, and is becoming popular as a way of cutting costs and increasing productivity. One such example is found at British Telecom. BT general counsel Chris Fowler explains: "...all requests for legal work within GS [BT's Global Services] come in through a web-based system and go directly to UnitedLex, which evaluates the request based on complexity; more complex tasks are passed to the in-house legal team in the UK while low-value, high-volume, repeatable tasks stay with UnitedLex".[6]

Technology

Technology is integral to a discussion about innovation and creativity; it has become ubiquitous and plays an integral role in every aspect of an individual's life. The founder and CEO of Dell Inc, Michael Dell, famously said: "Technology is about enabling human potential." We cannot underestimate the power of technology and its usefulness in the innovation ecosystem. One of the key areas that in-house legal counsel focus on in order to reduce the reactive work is to deliver regular training to clients on different topics – for example, boilerplate terms on customer and distribution contracts, playbooks, policies, operational processes, tools, and self-help flowcharts and wizards. The training and the transfer of knowledge – and accountability – from the legal team to the sales teams and support functions will transform these individuals into legal and compliance evangelists. As evangelists, they will educate their peers, customers, vendors, and partners to operate within the legal parameters set out in the documents listed above.

When it comes to delivering that training, what choices do we have as in-house counsel when there is a huge training need across the country or regions? We could deliver face-to-face training, which would require money and time. An alternative is online training delivered through e-learning platforms, videos, podcasts, or mobile applications. The latter requires time and money too, but the fact that it is created for repeated use, for audiences locally and globally, makes the return on investment a compelling business case while at the same time it enables us to monitor the attendance and completion of the training programs.

Opportunities to innovate

> *"Still, there is no escaping the fact that there is more to do with less time, less money and fewer people."* Richard G. Stock, *Inside Counsel*

Utilizing resources

Legal counsel have certain resources to maximize our competency as effective lawyers. These include administrative and paralegal support, data analysts, investigators, translators, and more or less generous budgets for IT and outside counsel spend. The question is whether limited resources translate to limited innovation. An interesting perspective on this issue can be found in a book entitled *Jugaad Innovation*,[7] in which the authors have approached innovation from a frugal perspective in the face of resource constraints. As long as we have the culture of innovation, we can charge ahead to do things in a new way through the "do-it-yourself" method: cheap, quick, and simple innovation.

To enable us to discharge fully our responsibilities we must be prepared to be innovative in our day-to-day work, which will free up our time to attend to the areas that pose the highest risk in other parts of the business. Being proactive and undertaking preventative work requires time for reflection, and if we are busy being reactive we may "lose sight of the shore". As general legal counsel, the neglect of the proactive part of our role could warp our professional outlook and career development. As the saying goes, "necessity is the mother of all invention" – since we understand the problem or the challenge, we can apply a new vision or perspective to a fundamental problem that improves on processes, technology, or costs.[8] If we are sitting at the decision-making table of the business leaders, business typically welcomes cutting-edge ideas from legal to ensure that risks are mitigated and it is legally compliant when products are sold into new markets, while still keeping the cost down.

Legal counsel have opportunities to innovate even when there are limited means to apply creativity. For example, in the application of the strict interpretation of the law in a given situation, legal advice could be communicated to clients in a creative manner. There are references to legal departments using social media, whether internal platforms such as Salesforce.com or external platforms like Facebook and Twitter, to communicate legal updates to their masses of employees and contractors in a bid to reduce email churn.[9] These bursts of legal updates in bite-sized chunks capture the attention of the busy audience of sales makers and employees at large because they are delivered in a short and targeted way. The power of social media in communicating in a one-to-many forum is effective.

Innovation to drive value

Furthermore, we have to manage the outside counsel budgets and build relationships with the outside counsel. Law schools have not trained us to operate businesses and become commercially savvy; neither is an MBA a necessary prerequisite to be a general legal counsel. However, we need to find ways to become better at controlling outside counsel costs. Law firms have begun to offer capped fees, value-based fees, fixed fees, success-based fees, and other alternatives to the billable hour for specific matters. Sometimes, law firms are open to a hybrid model in which a percentage of the fee is based on the hourly rate and the rest is contingent on the outcome of the matter. As legal counsel, we must be willing to innovate and to care about driving the most competitive rates for a specific matter. Negotiating an alternative fee arrangement (AFA) may create a sense of vulnerability because AFAs are still not commonplace within many of the top-tier firms today, but it starts with one small step from the legal counsel – willingness to innovate.

As fundamental as it is to managing the external spend with our outside counsel, innovation can be found in other parts of the relationship with the law firm. In the following paragraphs we will see how innovation can be applied in areas other than costs:

1. Alternatives to the request for proposal (RFP) process for selection of law firms; and
2. Access to previously issued legal advice.

Alternatives to the RFP process

When reduction of outside counsel fees is the tone set from the top in in-house legal departments, legal counsel who procure legal services for their organizations use RFPs to drive better pricing from the bidding law firms. The whole process starts with issuing the RFP, then evaluating the responses, and selecting the law firm. Nothing in this process involves the technical assessment of the law firm and its lawyers. The question-and-answer sessions and customer testimonials will give us an insight into the capability of the firm and its priorities, but it is not enough to test it on its competency. We could gauge its competency by giving the firm some paid work to assess the quality of its technical knowledge, speed of response, and so on, and measure other metrics that we would use to score the response.

Are your clients considering replacing or supplementing the traditional RFP process? At Dell, we asked the firms that aspired to provide legal services to our company in one country to spend two to three days in our local office on a non-paid basis to assess key risk areas in our local business. After a series of interviews with key functions, such as HR, marketing, and trade, each firm produced a report setting out its views on key risk areas, and recommendations. The report gave us a clear picture of the law firms' competency and capability from different angles – the depth of technical knowledge, pragmatism in the advice, and many other relevant areas. At this point, we had insight into their technical skills from a practical perspective and we could focus on the remainder of the RFP process, which was to apply the scorecard metrics to the other parts of the procurement of legal services exercise, such as value-added services, fees, and international presence. Needless to say, the reports themselves were great resources!

Access to previously issued legal advice

One of the first tasks of an incoming in-house counsel taking over from a predecessor will be to gain access to all the previously issued advice from outside counsel. Unless the organization has a document management system that stores outside counsel advice, the incoming counsel will tend to rely on their predecessor to forward the historical advice; this is the case at Dell. This, of course, assumes that the outgoing lawyer had a management system to store the advice and backed up that advice. As long as we exercise caution, the previously issued advice is a valuable resource to reduce the duplication of instruction to outside counsel.

Alternatively, the bigger law firms are now starting to offer web-based portals that store all of the historical legal opinions and advice. It is an excellent inter-organizational bridge because it provides access to the advice not only to the incoming legal counsel, but also to all other lawyers within the organization.[10] This reduces cycle time as we have easy access to historical advice, and it helps us control our costs with outside counsel.

Both of these innovation examples target the controlling of outside counsel spend, doing more with less, optimizing the resources of the organization without weakening our legal role or our duty to our internal clients, and building our relationships with our outside counsel through innovative approaches.

Tools for innovation

> *"Genius is one percent inspiration, and ninety-nine percent perspiration."* Thomas Edison

Have you ever wondered how we can stimulate innovative ideas? Unless a light bulb moment occurs or periods of reflection give rise to an idea, generating that idea is no easy feat. Some help is needed!

In my previous publications I have considered the notion that, as in-house counsel, we can learn from others who have gone before us in different industries, business functions, or international standard bodies, as the information is widely available on the internet.[11] There are plenty of toolkits that provide guidance on ways in which we can produce innovative ideas that deliver efficiency and cost savings. Most of us have tried one or more of the following methodologies: brainstorming; Six Sigma[12] for Lean law; the Kaizen approach to eliminate waste; the fishbone cause-and-effect diagram; the affinity diagram; or, most recently, crowdsourcing.

In fact, in Dell, the legal innovation team organized a global legal hackathon – similar to the UK's *Dragon's Den* TV show for aspiring entrepreneurs – across its four global regional legal teams to stir the creative streaks in the team members. The result was about 30 innovative solutions for various problem statements. The fishbone cause-and-effect diagram is a powerful tool for problem-solving, too, in a team environment. The team will define the problem statement, and identify all the contributing causes of the problem. Once the causes are identified, they will conduct a root cause analysis to establish what is causing each issue and take steps to eliminate it. Another positive by-product of this problem-solving approach is that engaging team members in developing the solution automatically increases the buy-in to the changes which have to be implemented.

One toolkit that legal departments have rarely discussed is TRIZ.[13] Engineers and research scientists in the technology and manufacturing sector use TRIZ principles as a creative problem-solving technique; TRIZ is derived from the study of patterns in past inventions and patents. Karen Gadd, in her book *TRIZ for Engineers: Enabling Inventive Problem Solving*,[14] explains the TRIZ methodology as a toolkit to guide engineers to understand their problem, articulate their ideal outcome, and then, by using data, logic, and research within TRIZ, develop an innovative solution. While TRIZ may not have been used widely by lawyers, Lilly Haines-Gadd says: "TRIZ is an attempt to try to cut across different disciplines and 'bottle' the fundamental logic of problem solving for everyone no matter what their job, specialty or area of expertise."[15] In-house counsel have hope! We can use TRIZ-based problem solving capabilities to develop innovative ideas. TRIZ has a number of toolkits and each one is suitable for a particular type of situation or problem.

One of my favorites is "40 principles"; it means there are 40 different ways of solving a physical or technical contradiction. A physical contradiction exists when we want opposite solutions. An example of physical contradiction is that training our sales teams comprehensively would take a long preparation time, but we want to deliver it in the minimum time. A technical contradiction is where we improve something, but the improvement also attracts something negative. An example of a technical contradiction in our industry is training – training our clients reduces compliance risks (good), but keeps our sales makers away from selling (bad).16

The advantage with the 40 inventive principles is that we can use the principles to eliminate contradictions in a solution – there is no need to choose between the good and bad solution; we can have both opposites or the improvement and the negative as a good solution. But first we have to understand the problem and define the ideal outcome. The common inventive principles are:

- Segmentation – for example, an intake process for allocation of work to a different category of legal team members;
- Self-service – for example, an automated triage on the web with questions and answers for frequently asked questions; and
- The other way around – for example, instead of a legal department storing its outside counsel advice, the outside counsel could provide access rights to a web-based database containing the advice, stored in a structured and systematic arrangement.

The Oxford Creativity TRIZ principles present a clear problem-solving technique. This includes: defining the ideal outcome and seeking ideas for ideal solutions; identifying, and seeking available resources to provide, the main functions of those ideal solutions; and using the inventive principles to eliminate any contradictions in order to produce an innovative idea that can be put into production. One of the 40 inventive principles is to copy – for example, the in-house counsel can copy the engineer's ways of developing an invention using the TRIZ methods.

Some of the ideas that have been implemented in legal departments – such as automation of templates, standardization of routine work, automation of self-triage using decision trees, e-learning and interactive training, dynamic heat maps, contract generators, and mobile applications – are good examples of innovation and I would not be surprised if each of them was a TRIZ-inspired creation!

Conclusion

> *"I think that's the single best piece of advice: constantly think about how you could be doing things better, and questioning yourself."* Elon Musk, CEO of Tesla

Pressures on cost savings, advances in technology, and access to top talent from all different parts of the world have justified embracing innovation and creativity as a way to run lean legal departments, while maintaining maximum compliance in the business. In this chapter we have looked at several ways in which in-house legal departments can promote and foster innovation, through the combined forces of forward-thinking leadership and a change in culture and the mindsets of the legal team members. For both in-house and outside counsel, innovation and creativity starts in law school; poring over the law books, case law, and statutes, and understanding their application to the exam questions, requires some problem solving skills – albeit basic skills. The structures of the law curriculum provide a good foundation on which to develop complex problem-solving skills; however, unless we are motivated and curious to ask "why", "what", and "how" when faced with a problem, and then do something about it, innovation will simply be a buzzword. In-house legal departments have proven to be as successful as law firms in developing innovative business models that benefit their clients. A business's success hinges upon its ability to innovate and willingness to innovate; the same expectation applies to its legal department. Law firms' partnership with legal departments will drive a shared success in innovation in the legal industry as a whole.

References

1. This chapter is written based on my experiences and does not represent the views of my employer, Dell, except where I have cited Dell.
2. Sloane, P., "What is the difference between innovation and creativity?", www.innovationexcellence.com, 7 June 2010. See http://www.innovationexcellence.com/blog/2010/06/07/what-is-the-difference-between-innovation-and-creativity/.

3. Bloom, B. S.; Engelhart, M. D.; Furst, E. J.; Hill, W. H.; Krathwohl, D. R., *Taxonomy of Educational Objectives: The Classification of Educational Goals. Handbook I: Cognitive Domain.* New York: David McKay Company, 1956.
4. Hill, L. A., Brandeau, G., Truelove, E. and Lineback, K., *Collective Genius: The Art and Practice of Creating Innovation*, Boston: Harvard Business School Publishing, 2014.
5. Verganti, R., "The innovative power of criticism", *Harvard Business Review*, Jan-Feb 2016.
6. Chris Fowler, General Counsel, UK, British Telecom, www.acc.com/valuechallenge/valuechamps/2013champ_profilebt.cfm.
7. Radjou, N., Prabhu, J. and Ahuja, S., *Jugaad Innovation: Think Frugal, Be Flexible, Generate Breakthrough Growth*, California: Jossey-Bass, 2012.
8. See https://www.linkedin.com/pulse/embracing-innovation-deepa-tharmaraj?trk=mp-reader-card.
9. Example of micro-blogging and instant messaging by China State Construction, 2013 ACC Value Champion: https://www.acc.com/valuechallenge/valuechamps/2013champ_profilechinastate.cfm.
10. In some countries, the concept of legal and litigation privilege and attorney-client privilege may prevent open access of certain advice to legal counsel outside the country it was issued from. Please exercise with caution. In the *Harvard Business Review* article "Meeting the challenge of disruptive change" (March-April 2000), Clayton M. Christensen and Michael Overdorf have added that in addition to resources and process, the company's values affect what an organization can and cannot do for disruptive innovation.
11. www.theoath-me.com/s/in-house-view-embracing-innovation.
12. A renowned author who speaks and writes regularly on this topic is Ken Grady, who is the Lean Law Evangelist for Seyfarth Shaw LLP.
13. Russian acronym for the "theory of inventive problem solving" developed by G.S. Altshuller and his colleagues in the former USSR between 1946 and 1985.
14. Gadd, K., *TRIZ for Engineers: Enabling Inventive Problem Solving*, Sussex: John Wiley & Sons, 2011.
15. Haines-Gadd, L., *TRIZ for Dummies*, Chichester: John Wiley & Sons, 2016.
16. See www.mindtools.com/pages/article/newCT_92.htm.

Part 2:
Case Studies

Case study 1:
Fast forward – Driving top-line revenue for your law firm

By Jill Weber, chief marketing and business development officer at Stinson Leonard Street LLP

About Stinson Leonard Street

Stinson Leonard Street LLP provides sophisticated transactional and litigation services to clients ranging from individuals and privately held enterprises to national companies and international corporations. We blend a collaborative environment, innovative project management, and deep legal knowledge to deliver value and a rewarding experience to our clients.

In an increasingly competitive legal environment, managing partners are responsible for:

- Growing top-line revenue for the firm;
- Strengthening the firm so that it will continue to grow and thrive in the future; and
- Identifying and supporting the next generation of firm leaders.

This chapter shares the case study of a successful business development program that achieves all three of these goals.

Stinson Leonard Street's Fast Forward® program[1] provides attorneys with a systematic approach to business development, helping them build larger and more durable practices for years to come. Over the past 12 years, 87 partners have participated in one of six two-year programs the firm has sponsored. The initial group of 20 Fast Forward participants grew their practices by $7.5 million in the aggregate (a 79 percent increase) over a two-year period. Nine of those initial participants today have significant and sustainable practices, and 90 percent of participants in the program have achieved fee growth of some kind.

In this chapter we will provide an overview of the Fast Forward program, highlighting:

- The revenue-generating strategy;
- The core program elements that are key to the success of this integrated approach;
- The selection criteria any managing partner can use in identifying high-potential partners for business development training and coaching;
- The primary benefits for attorneys who have participated in the program;
- A high-level summary of results, including both financial metrics and subjective feedback from program participants; and
- The top 10 Fast Forward takeaways for managing partners.

An innovative idea

In 2003, our firm's then managing partner had an idea. He wanted to generate an additional $10 million in incremental revenue for the firm, and he decided he could achieve this goal by asking 20 partners to agree to grow their practices by $500,000 each over a two-year period. When I joined the firm, he asked me to develop a program to accomplish this objective.

We started the process using competitive intelligence to identify best practices from other law firms for business development initiatives to support individual attorney revenue growth goals. We also looked outside the legal industry for best practices used with traditional sales forces – for example, in software or pharmaceutical sales.

Within the legal industry, we identified several core tactics being used by law firms – partner business plans, professional coaches outside of the law firm, business development training programs – but found that no one was bringing these elements together into a cohesive program with a clearly articulated goal. We also identified two drawbacks to traditional coaching programs:

- Many coaching programs are limited in scope/time – the coach worked with the attorney for just six to 12 months, limiting the time available to modify business development behavior and create good habits; and
- Most business development coaching is a lonely experience, with attorneys working one-on-one with a coach but not sharing ideas or best practices with other peers.

Outside the legal industry, we found two core elements of traditional sales programs that did not exist in law firms:

- Traditional sales organizations are transparent in sharing data with the sales force. Sales "quotas" are communicated from senior leadership, and sales professionals' performance against those measures are regularly monitored and reported; and
- Incentives for outstanding sales achievement are prominent and transparent – for example, the "President's Club" trip or other financial rewards.

We decided to incorporate both elements into our law firm's program.

An integrated approach

While the research was helpful in identifying several standalone best practices, we determined that integrating the most successful practices into a cohesive whole would differentiate our program from others in the market. We established the following core program elements.

Required commitment

The program represents a significant investment of the firm's resources. In return, we ask participating attorneys to make a significant commitment of time and effort to the program.

Individual business plan

Participants develop personalized business plans, tailored to each attorney's specific area of practice, client base, and personal marketing strengths and preferences.

One-on-one coaching

We engaged two outside coaches to provide personalized coaching to the participants. The coaches' role included:

- Assisting the participant in developing their individual business plan;
- Providing monthly coaching calls, to counsel and offer ideas;
- Holding participants accountable; and
- Serving as a sounding board for pitches and client meetings.

Educational curriculum

In addition to the personalized monthly coaching calls, the collective group participates in a series of business development training programs. We decided the educational curriculum would consist of two parts:

- Educational presentations on topics of interest to the participants (e.g. preparing for a client/prospect meeting, maximizing participation in industry/trade association conferences, etc.); and
- Sharing of ideas among participants.

Incentives

We established tiered rewards for success based on results. Those who achieved the $500,000 revenue growth goal over two years would receive a four-day, three-night trip with their spouse to any Ritz-Carlton in the United States, including airfare, lodging, meals and childcare expenses. Smaller rewards were offered for results at lower levels of revenue growth.

Measurement

Program participants and their coaches would complete monthly financial reports tracking progress against their stated revenue goals. Financial results would be shared with the firm's leadership team on an annual basis. Participant surveys would be conducted at six months, one year, and at the conclusion of the two-year program to gather direct feedback from program participants.

Accountability

Participants commit to a specific revenue goal and that goal is shared not only with their outside coaches but also with the firm's chief marketing and business development officer (CMBDO) and leadership team. Educational programs emphasize personal accountability, providing a forum for the participants to update one another on prior months' activities.

Brand identity

We created a brand identity for the program, naming it "Fast Forward" as the program was designed to help participants accelerate their revenues with a more systematic approach to business development.

A focused approach

Once the program design was complete, we turned to the selection of candidates for the program. Initially, our plan was to open the program to all partners, asking them to submit a nomination form that provided both quantitative (past revenue history, key clients) and qualitative (personal motivation, long-term business development goals) criteria. After developing the initial nomination form and looking at potential candidates, we determined that the nominations process might serve as a drawback to highly motivated partners who were already busy with billable hours and may not see the immediate benefit to participating in this new program. We decided to take a different approach, asking our firm's business development committee to select participants for the initial program.

To assist the committee in evaluating and identifying potential program participants, we established selection criteria for the program. While criteria for each firm will vary depending upon program goals, our selection criteria included the following categories:

Lawyer classification

While the program could benefit lawyers ranging from senior associates to senior partners, we focused on partners who had not yet achieved significant, sustainable business development success.

Business development experience

We focused on partners who had demonstrated an ability to generate business, either inside the firm (great client service to partners and the clients they serve) or outside the firm (great contacts or network, involvement in an industry association, or a modest book of business).

Revenue range

We identified a target range of existing revenue for consideration, with a minimum revenue requirement as well as a maximum.

Existing network of contacts

To successfully create and implement an individual business plan, partners needed to have a strong existing network of clients, prospects, referral sources, and other contacts. Those looking to build a network were not a target for the program.

Personally motivated

After implementing six two-year Fast Forward programs, we have learned that personal motivation is key to success in the program. High resilience and low skepticism are critical factors that influence program outcomes.

The power of first impressions

In a world driven by smartphones and email, face-to-face communications still reign supreme when building relationships. We avoided the blanket email invitation and opted for a personalized approach. A key business generator and the firm's CMBDO met with each prospective participant individually, in person, to discuss the scope of the program and extend an invitation to be part of the program. The face-to-face invitation process not only provided an opportunity to candidly assess attorney interest and answer questions, it also reinforced accountability for the participants.

The kick-off meeting with all participants also represented an opportunity to build relationships and reinforce accountability. While many law firms host meetings over informal lunches in their offices, we opted for an off-site reception in a private room at an upscale restaurant. Firm leaders participated in the kick-off meeting, communicating the firm's support and oversight of the program.

The "Valley of Despair"

After implementing the Fast Forward program for more than a decade, we have found that the partners who benefit most from participation in the program are those who are in the "Valley of Despair". Most often, these are young partners who were very successful associates but have experienced a decline in billable hours as they transitioned from associate to partner, and the work their fellow partners formerly assigned to them is now going to other associates. The other partners expect them to find their own work now that they are partners, but these newer partners were so busy serving the needs of other partners and clients as associates that they didn't focus on business development. No matter how often you talk with associates about the importance of building business development skills to be successful, it doesn't hit home until they become a partner.

The Fast Forward program delivers several benefits to newer partners who find themselves in the "Valley of Despair". The program offers:

- A systematic approach to business development;
- The opportunity to focus energy on those business development activities most likely to generate success;
- Greater autonomy and independence (i.e. not relying on others to "feed" you);
- Opportunities to build relationships both within the firm (partners in other practice areas and offices) and within the community (industry/trade associations);
- Knowledge about other practice areas to assist in cross-selling; and
- A trusted peer group to share ideas and jointly approach clients and prospects.

Results

At the end of two years, the 20 participants in the firm's initial Fast Forward program achieved a collective revenue growth of $7.5 million based on a program investment of $150,000. In addition, program participants achieved an average fee-receipts growth rate six times higher than the average for their peer group. More important, a decade later, nine of the participants in the initial program have sustainable and significant books of business, many representing key institutional clients.

In addition to the financial metrics, we conduct a survey of all participants at the end of each program. The subjective feedback we receive is as important as the objective results. We find that program participants are more focused, more engaged, and more invested in business development going forward. The Fast Forward program helps to create effective, sustainable habits that benefit the attorneys – and the firm – for years to come. Following are direct quotes from Fast Forward participant surveys:

- "It keeps me focused on the most important and achievable marketing objectives."
- "This program should be sold as the 'inevitable' steps for having a successful practice, not an option."
- "The program pushes me to do things I otherwise wouldn't make time for."
- "It facilitates and encourages cross-marketing better than any other activities I've seen the firm undertake."
- "Participation has caused me to focus on existing clients… has allowed me to gain a better understanding of client needs and has encouraged me to actually ask for opportunities to expand our current client service."
- "Fewer seminars; more one-on-one contacts."
- "I have more regular contact with potential clients and opinion makers."

More important than the financial results or subjective feedback, however, is the fact that the program creates an annuity for the firm. We modify attorney behavior, changing how the attorneys think about, focus on, and implement business development activities. Our Fast Forward "graduates" are more engaged in cross-selling, more disciplined about their business plans, and more connected to their peers than they were when they started in the program. The program impact can't just be measured at the end of two years – it can best be measured in 10 or 20 years when we look at the client base, cross-selling, and leadership of past program participants.

A packaged product

After dozens of presentations at industry programs across the country, and calls and interest from managing partners and marketing professionals who sought to emulate the program at their own firms, we decided to package core elements of the program and sell it to other law firms. We have implemented it at law firms and accounting firms, and the implementation process in different environments helps to refine and enhance the program for the future.

Top 10 takeaways for managing partners

As we reflect on the program's evolution and success, we've identified 10 key takeaways to share with managing partners:

1. **It's a marathon, not a sprint**. Business development programs are not "one and done". Invest for the future;
2. **Think team. Individual coaching is isolating**. Creating a group to share ideas and best practices maximizes the value of the coaching investment;
3. **Be flexible**. We adapt the program elements and training curriculum to meet the unique needs of each group of attorneys as they join the program;
4. **Create a memorable brand**. A program brand enhances the credibility of the initiative and raises visibility with future participants;

5. **Provide incentives**. As young partners are building their practices, compensation will be a lagging indicator until they have built a substantial book of business. Create additional opportunities for incentives and rewards to recognize disciplined, focused business development activity;
6. **What gets measured gets done**. Set quantifiable goals, report regularly, analyze rigorously, and be transparent;
7. **Facilitate feedback**. Once you've received the feedback, share the aggregate results with participants and leadership, and modify the program accordingly;
8. **Create a pilot program**. Test and refine with an initial group of willing participants;
9. **Be prepared for the "Valley of Despair"**. We have found that enthusiastic participants at the program outset can lose motivation as they begin to implement their plans and realize just how much work is required to build a practice. Be prepared to provide leadership support not just at the outset, but as the program evolves; and
10. **Praise efforts, not only results, publicly**. We applaud innovation and learn from mistakes. Some of our best ideas have come from Fast Forward program participants exploring different business development activities to see what works, and what doesn't.

Reference

1. Fast Forward is a registered trademark of Deinard Enterprises LLC.

Case study 2:
Stewarts Law's organic growth strategy

By John Cahill, managing partner and co-founder of Stewarts Law LLP

About Stewarts Law

We like to think that Stewarts Law is different. We specialize in high-value and complex disputes. Our track record of winning for our clients has supported our success and helped us become the UK's largest litigation-only law firm. Our focus on litigation-only (our product) has, when combined with specialist expertise (our people), been the main driver for our profitability.

Our product

From the outset it was my intention that Stewarts Law should concentrate on complex high-value disputes, many with an international element. When I took over as managing partner 15 years ago, the firm was best known for its personal injury work. I continued this focus, but differentiated it from those of competing firms by concentrating almost entirely on the most extreme catastrophic injury cases. In personal injury, only one percent of claims are for more than £1 million and those are the cases we focused on. With catastrophic injuries come other claims for clinical negligence – people going into hospital with terrible injuries and having the double whammy of being poorly treated when they get there. So we followed the same strategy with that. Over the past two years, the firm has resolved around 150 injury cases and recovered around £300 million, an average of £2 million per client.

Another injury-related expansion took us into aviation and travel litigation. The injury group is now regarded externally as the standout group in the UK for claimant catastrophic injury work.[1]

The high-value model has now gone well beyond injury bolt-ons. In 2008 we moved into divorce and family. Our aim was to act for high net worth individuals only. We set out to rival the very best firms in London in five years, and we have done that. Our typical divorce client has a case involving several potential jurisdictions and assets worth more than £50 million.

In addition to our injury and divorce departments, we now have a very substantial commercial litigation department (around 40 lawyers). Newer departments include competition litigation, employment, international arbitration, and tax litigation. Trust litigation is our latest practice area. Overall, our commercial disputes work currently accounts for nearly 50 percent of everything we do, an evolution that has long been in the planning.

The careful and often innovative strategic positioning of the individual departments operating from our London and Leeds offices differentiates us from our competitors, and helps each department to compete successfully for the very best work in its chosen sector and deliver value to clients.

Over the course of the next five years it is envisaged that the core strategic positioning of the firm will evolve but remain fundamentally unchanged, with growth coming from the addition of new lawyers in those practice areas best placed for expansion, the addition of new practice areas, increased internationalization through newly targeted international alliances, and the successful application of innovative funding models.

Our people

The thing is, it is not just about skill sets – it is about fit. We have 135 qualified partners and lawyers at the moment and I have personally interviewed and approved the appointment of all of them. When we bring in another, the first question in my mind is always: "How well will they fit with the others?" To answer that you need to have one person with an overview and, for now, that person is me.

The emphasis on fit runs all the way through Stewarts Law, from bottom to top. In 2015 the firm took on four new trainees, all recruited from our paralegal staff. There were 49 applicants for the places. Many other firms would have delegated tests and interviews to the human resources department. Here the process is run by two equity partners, with me involved in the final selection from a shortlist.

I asked someone to visit the stationery shop, Ryman, and come back with eight things that cost under £1 each; he bought an HB pencil, a fluff roller, a battery-powered mini fan, a tube of glue, and various other things like that. The eight shortlisted finalists were asked to go to the back of the interview room and agree amongst themselves who would defend which object as being the most innovative.

When they had done their sales pitches on their chosen objects, I gave each of them 10 minutes to write a poem about Stewarts Law. As it happens, Tom, who won the pitch (the one who chose the pencil), was also the winner of the poetry round. He wrote a haiku: "In any weather – Stewarts Law fights complex claims – winning for clients." It may not be an Ezra Pound poem, but it does sum us up pretty well in 17 syllables.

This year, seven new trainees have been appointed with similar rigor applied to the interview process.

Our profitability

The firm aims to achieve growth which is sustainable and smart. Our focus is on net profit, not revenue. Actual net profitability firm-wide has averaged around 43 percent in the last five years. Our current net profitability goal (post fixed partner profit shares) is 45 percent. To help us achieve our profitability goals I have developed the "five filters" test, which can be summarized as:

- High net profit (overall target of 45 percent benchmarked for different departments);
- High realization rates (target of between 90–120 percent, benchmarked for different departments depending on funding types);
- Departmental income self-funding its equity partners;
- Value thresholds for new business; and
- Maintaining an appropriate balance between contingent and non-contingent cases to enable risk-taking in tandem with strong cash flow.

The correct pricing of our legal services will remain a key component to the optimization of net profit and realization rates. The concept of departmental income self-funding equity partners is a simple one, which is set out in our lockstep policy. The policy makes it clear that the overall financial performance of a department will be a significant consideration when reviewing partner entry into lockstep. Departments are broadly expected to generate a sufficient profit to meet their respective unit allocation and, in addition, a sum sufficient to contribute to non-departmentally based equity partners. Value bars or thresholds have been introduced to help ensure that the criteria for accepting new business are met so that the cases we accept are consistent with our strategic objectives. The aim is to increase the bars over time as the greatest proportion of the firm's fees is derived from our highest value and most complex cases. Maintaining a balance between contingent and non-contingent cases is a developing theme. As part of the rapid growth the firm has witnessed in the last five years, the equity partners have been mindful of the need to balance monthly billing work, which represents a low risk of recovery, with contingent work of one kind or another, which represents a higher risk of recovery.

To support the expansion of our contingent work, much time has been spent in developing alternative funding mechanisms.

These include bespoke conditional fee (CFA) and damages-based (DBA) agreements, and new after the event (ATE) products. The firm also intends to increase the amount by which it funds work from its own balance sheet.

Improving product, people, and profitability

- Offer something different – differentiation is key in today's legal market;
- Do not just hand over recruitment to HR;
- Remember, it is not just about skill sets, it is about fit; and
- Build in a correlation between departmental profit and equity allocation.

The other stuff

Of course, there are a lot of other less tangible factors, which together are important in creating the right environment to succeed. At the outset, it is essential to design a physical environment where individuals will thrive and to assert core values (in our case teamwork, innovation, manners, and excellence), which will provide a behavioral framework. Having core values is incredibly important for all organizations. Adhering to them is even more important and this requires constant repetition and practical examples of adherence on a weekly basis.

Not surprisingly, our core values are carried over into our KPIs for entry to equity. The KPIs we measure are profitability, business development, and good citizenship. The latter, as with teamwork and manners, encourages the kind of behavior we want to foster within the firm. Partners are required to look up from their desks and think about what they can do to help others in the firm. Full equity is not achievable without a good score on citizenship.

Excellence is, of course, a common value to espouse. The high level of expertise among our leading lawyers, combined with our exclusive focus on complex and high value litigation, means we have a valuable knowledge pool that we seek to tap into and disseminate internally. Our knowledge management and compliance team has no fee-earning duties and so is better able to focus on assisting our fee earners to produce a consistently good work product.

Innovation at Stewarts Law is important as a differentiator. Examples include: being litigation-only; departments strategically positioned to offer competitive advantage; strategies around case capture; case plans offering alternative bespoke solutions to best fit our clients' goals and expectations; and innovative funding solutions which enable us to risk-share alongside our clients.

At Stewarts Law we have a "blueprint", which we review annually and which represents more than anything a combination of concepts, methods, and values that have been used to good effect and which we plan to continue to use. Many of the concepts in the blueprint have been touched upon in this case study. One that has not, and which deserves mention, is the importance of management making decisions quickly. The 80/20 rule will be familiar to most, and like many other organizations we aim to be right at least 80 percent of the time. This rule assists us in making decisions quickly and acting on them quickly. This can also include cutting losses when things do not go entirely to plan!

The results

When I took over as managing partner in the year 2000, our turnover was just over £3 million. At the time of writing, our draft management accounts show a turnover for the 2015/2016 financial year of around £63 million. This £60 million increase in revenue over 15 years means that we have been one of the fastest growing law firms in the UK over that period. Although we are ranked just outside the top 50 law firms in the UK, we are well in the top 10 for profitability.[2]

We have not done any of this by being complacent. It has been very hard work, actually. Fun, too, and challenging. But it did not just happen by accident. We had a clear vision to be the leading litigation firm in our chosen practice areas, employing the very best partners and staff, delivering high quality litigation, and achieving sustainable and smart growth.

Whether or not a strategy of merger/acquisition, as opposed to our current model of largely organic growth, could support the firm's ambition is a question that has been and will continue to be asked from time to time. An important consideration will be whether the target itself could pass the "five filters" test. Any potential merger partner would first need to be a litigation-only business, contain the right people, offer well-regarded and complimentary services/products, and, finally, be sufficiently profitable. The firm remains open to the concept of merger/acquisition should the right opportunity present itself in the future, either inside or outside the UK.

Postscript

Aspiring to a 45 percent profit margin is a good aspiration to have, not least if alongside it sits a willingness to support charitable activities. In 2010 we set up the Stewarts Law Foundation (SLF). Over the last six years we have given over £3 million to numerous deserving causes.

One charity we have supported is the Access to Justice Foundation (ATJF). The ATJF was set up to receive and distribute funds to facilitate and support the provision of free legal advice and assistance to those who need it most. The SLF feels strongly that it is essential to maintain access to justice, the mark of any civilized society, particularly at a time of very substantial funding cuts in the sector. To quote Martha de la Roche of ATJF: "The SLF support over the last few years has been absolutely vital in helping keep community law centers open."

The Foundation is important to our partners and to our staff as it reinforces the message that profitability is a good goal to have, especially if a proportion of those profits can support others less fortunate than ourselves.

References

1. According to *Legal 500*.
2. See: http://www.lawgazette.co.uk/news/financial-results/.

Case study 3:
The LP Way – A revenue growth strategy

By Angela Hickey, executive director at Levenfeld Pearlstein LLC

About Levenfeld Pearlstein LLC

Twice recognized by the *National Law Journal* as one of the nation's most innovative mid-sized law firms, Chicago-based Levenfeld Pearlstein LLC (LP) provides legal and business counsel to sophisticated clients across a broad range of corporate, tax, real estate, and litigation matters. LP works with clients to understand the full impact of the law on their businesses and proactively addresses their legal issues so that they can quickly return to doing what they do best.

What is the LP Way?

It is a widely known and accepted business principle that in any industry most new revenue is generated from existing clients or leads. A primary revenue growth strategy at LP is to create a consistent and unparalleled client experience as a means to generate referrals for new business from existing clients. Delivering a positive client *experience* is different and more complex than providing good or even excellent client *service*. Client service is transactional and often relies upon individual interpretation of what good service is. Client experience is comprehensive and occurs only when there is a structure to support it.

The LP Way™ is a five-step process designed to deliver an exceptional experience for clients of LP. It is based on many years of lessons learned and proven business disciplines rolled into a single and simplified approach that has become a common language at LP. It works because it is understood and embraced by everyone in the law firm. Even more important than understanding the process, people at all levels of the firm understand *why* it is necessary – to create a consistent and unparalleled client experience. When people understand why they are doing something and how it is connected to the strategy, they become empowered and are inclined to embrace it.

People are busy and cannot easily absorb a complicated strategy on top of their daily responsibilities. The LP Way steps are intentionally and deceivingly simple. It is also by design that the LP Way is presented as steps and not as a circle or some other depiction. Each step must occur in order and cannot be skipped. The steps build upon each other to create the intended client experience (see Figure 1).

At the essence of any client-centric business strategy is a decentralization of ownership of the client experience. Levenfeld Pearlstein has dedicated enormous energy into

Figure 1: The LP Way steps

communicating what the LP Way is, and why it is essential to the business strategy of the firm. At its launch in 2013, the LP Way was introduced by the executive committee, the highest governing body in the firm.

The roll-out

Each member of the executive committee received training in how to lead in-person, mixed group discussions. Groups were thoughtfully selected and intentionally mixed to include members from every level and practice group in the firm. The objectives of the launch meetings were clearly outlined:

- Help people understand the concept of the LP Way, that is, connect the dots – emphasizing connectivity and interdependence;
- Explore and understand where each person fits – help people envision and embrace their contribution; and
- Emphasize *why* the LP Way is important/necessary/critical, that is, the client experience.

Additionally, during the meetings, each member of the executive committee sought to identify "star contributors" to comprise a leading team to suggest ways to embed the LP Way into the firm. More on this later.

Prior to the LP Way rollout, the firm was already doing or trying to implement all of the things encompassed in the LP Way steps; however, these initiatives were seemingly disjointed and unconnected. The firm was trying to do too much in too many areas, and people either selected only what they wanted to do and/or began to disengage because they could not commit to everything expected of them. The LP Way brings everything together under a single structure and removes distractions and excuses by clearly showing the relationship of various firm initiatives and investments to the business strategy of building a client experience.

The LP Way steps in detail

Step 1: Attract and retain talented people

This step stems from the belief that everything begins with the right people. It is the first step because without the right people, even the best strategy cannot be executed. It is an idea inspired by Jim Collins in his book *Good to Great*[1] – getting the right people in the right seats on the bus. At LP, this includes everyone and not just attorneys or even just partners. Every single person associated with the firm, including strategic partners outside of the firm, plays an important role in creating client experience.

This first step emphasizes the importance of the firm's image in the marketplace. Talent is attracted to a firm whose brand resonates. An authentic image is created and maintained through vehicles such as branding, public relations, social media, corporate social responsibility, and the firm website. LP heavily incorporates video in branding endeavors and creates strategic relationships with outside partners to deliver the highest quality image. Many prospective hires (and clients, for that matter) are surprised to learn that LP is mid-sized given the firm's high quality image.

The recruiting approach at LP is targeted and deliberate. There is a target-based recruiting strategy with its own award-winning microsite. Potential hires are encouraged to understand the firm they are considering joining, including understanding the LP Way. It is a risk to be choosy in such a highly competitive war for talent, but a bad hire can be detrimental in so many ways and it is worth the time to find the right fit.

The approach to retention is also targeted and deliberate. A positive employee experience will lead to a positive client experience. The LP Way can only be delivered through people so it is essential that attorneys and staff at all levels feel respected and appreciated. The retention component of this first step transitions to the next step of leading by example.

Step 2: Lead by example

Talented people have options and will not stay in a toxic culture, no matter how well they are paid. The second LP Way step embodies the onboarding and cultural integration of the firm's non-negotiable values. There is an expectation that everyone in the firm lives up to those values.

The LP non-negotiable values are:

1. Clients first;
2. Personal growth and responsibility;
3. Collaboration; and
4. The "no asshole" rule.

There are no exceptions to the LP non-negotiable values. It is worth exploring each non-negotiable value individually. "Clients first" is about prioritization. The full order is: clients first, firm second, individuals in the firm last. When faced with a choice, people in the firm are expected to put the clients and the firm before themselves. The culture does not reward selfishness.

The second non-negotiable value of personal growth is about not resting on laurels. In order to remain sharp and relevant, each person is encouraged to continually challenge their personal comfort zone to stretch and to grow. Curiosity and lifetime learning are the foundation of innovation, and LP is a learning organization. There are many examples of successes and triumphs because of this value. It is not enough for each person to personally grow but each person must also help others to do so through training, mentoring, coaching, and sponsorship. This value encompasses personal responsibility. It is not someone else's job to lead by example. It is everyone's job to do so.

The non-negotiable value of collaboration is inherent in the firm's approach to serving clients. LP is not a collection of individual practitioners. Better outcomes occur when people work together than when they work alone. The best outcomes occur when those collaborating represent diverse perspectives and experiences. LP encourages collaboration in all endeavors, including in business development actions such as client and prospective client pitches. The goal is to create a bigger pie and not to bicker over the size of the pie slices.

The "no asshole" rule gets a lot of attention, particularly in an industry that is notorious for tolerating misbehaving partners who bring in a lot of business. There is no person better or lesser than another at LP. While everyone is allowed a bad day once in a while, chronic assholes are not tolerated. They are terminated, ideally before they cause too much damage to the culture.

These values belong to LP but they could be any values. The point of step 2 is not necessarily the values themselves but the expectation that everyone will walk the talk and lead by example when it comes to the values. Those on the inside of any organization know the difference between what a firm says and what a firm does. It is almost pointless to try to execute any further on the LP Way steps if the actions are not aligned with the values.

Step 3: Cultivate effective practice groups

Practice groups are the frontline of the client experience. This step is perhaps the most challenging of all steps to execute but it is worth the effort. Leading a practice group is a lot to ask of a lawyer whose formal training most likely did not include management or leadership training (this is why professional growth and personal responsibility in step 2 are a necessary prerequisite to step 3). Practice group leaders at LP receive dedicated training in change management, coaching, leadership, and other "soft" skills that are necessary to lead an LP practice group.

Leading any group effectively and getting the group to expose and address its areas for improvement requires vulnerability and trust. Trust is typically not a currency emphasized in law firms; however, in order to coalesce around the client experience, groups must be honest about who they are and how things are done. Collaboration is a hallmark of how LP and its practice groups operate. Collaboration is fostered both within and between practice areas. Crossing practice groups is the danger zone of client experience because if groups handle things differently, the client experience may suffer.

With an emphasis on client value and client experience, groups regularly discuss innovation, consistency, and process efficiency in the way work gets done. This often results in a single method or format for the entire group to adopt for various items. Personal style and habits are typical casualties of this step. It is the most difficult step to execute because it requires more personal change than the other steps.

LP has invested heavily in innovation in the delivery of client services. A manager of process improvement was hired in 2013 whose sole responsibility is to support practice groups in identifying processes ripe for improvement and to develop creative solutions for improving inefficient processes. This has led to a revamped process for compiling and delivering closing books, the development of a corporate entity database to automatically generate annual reports, and a dedicated client extranet platform, among many other projects. The changes are extremely well received by clients.[2] Process improvement requires experimentation and this requires failure. Failure is not something most attorneys embrace as a sign of progress. If practice groups do not provide a safe place to fail, then no one will ever try or suggest anything new.

Changing the way work gets done necessitates a change in the way work is priced (and vice versa). It is no secret that price is a pain point in the experience of most law firm clients. If lawyers are allowed to be inefficient in the way work gets done and then to charge by the hour for their inefficiency, the client winds up paying more for the work than is necessary. Clients recognize this and many law firms, including LP, feel the pressure from clients to lower cost. To lower cost without changing the way the work is done or who is doing it only reduces quality and margins.

LP partners are trained and coached in how to effectively scope, price, and manage engagements, and in how to initiate conversations about price with clients. LP believes that client value happens at the intersection of *p*rocess efficiency, strategic *p*ricing, and effective *p*roject management (P3). The "Ps" are heavily emphasized and embraced by the practice groups.

All LP attorneys, paralegals, and managers receive extensive project management training. Project management is emphasized as a skill that everyone should have rather than as a separate job that is someone else's responsibility to do. It is common to see attorney-led process mapping sessions to address and improve various processes in the firm.

This third step of the LP Way utilizes group and personal plans for goal achievement. Every attorney prepares an annual personal plan that is connected to an overall practice group plan. Plans are simple and are based on outcomes. They are published internally for all to see and serve as important accountability tools.

Step 4: Align support structure

Effective system alignment fosters the right behaviors. Support structures in law firms usually conjure images of typical back-office functions such as accounting and technology; however, there are many organizational systems that must align in order to effectively execute strategy. These include governance, development, reward, and support systems. The most important element in this step is alignment. Everything is connected and everything is moving in a law firm. If a system gets too far out of alignment, then the strategy, and in this case, the client experience, breaks down.

The governance system includes firm management and succession. Who is at the helm making decisions is something that matters to everyone in the firm. LP has three standing committees: executive, compensation, and promotion. There are transparent requirements and term limits for members of these committees. The uncertainty that surrounds succession planning can be a significant distraction in any business. It is impossible to focus on the client experience if the leaders of the firm are focused on self-preservation. At LP, no person may serve on a standing committee or as the managing partner beyond the age of 60. This is intended to keep the younger generation engaged and also to incentivize the older generation to properly train and provide opportunities for future leaders, decision makers, and client relationship managers in the firm.

A succession plan does not work if there is no one trained and capable to take the reins. The development systems incorporate business development, professional development, leadership development, and personal development. Heavy investment and attention is given to each of these often overlapping areas. LP uses a mix of inside and outside resources for training and coaching and relies upon an element of self-motivation to ensure execution.

The reward system includes promotion and compensation. The reward system holds the clearest and most visible opportunity for misalignment. These systems must not reward behaviors that do not conform to the non-negotiable values identified in step 2. This is literally "putting your money where your mouth is" when it comes to the LP Way strategy. The promotion system provides clear expectations and is secured by a system of checks and balances to guard against advancement of personal favorites as a primary driver. The compensation system also provides clear expectations; it is not formulaic; it incorporates a balanced scorecard approach; and it is completely transparent at the equity member level. People at all levels of the firm understand what is valued in the reward systems and what they must do to advance. Law firm compensation is an area that is often approached as if it is somehow independent from clients other than through a business origination link, but it is directly linked to client value and to client experience. The LP compensation approach looks far beyond the face value of origination in order to fully recognize a client's overall experience and connection to the firm. Relationships that are shared and cross into multiple firm areas create "stickiness" that is more valuable to both the client and to the firm than is a single point-to-point contact.

The support system includes human resources, knowledge management, records, technology, facilities, marketing, and accounting. So often, these functions are relegated as "back office" or less important than other areas of the firm, but the client experience can break down very easily if these systems are disengaged or unaligned. These functions at LP are built to support the client experience in many ways.

Human resources

HR ensures that recruiting, onboarding, and retention efforts are consistent with the LP Way. A colleague of mine refers to his HR department as the "human roadblock" department. Unfortunately, this can definitely be the case when HR is overly focused on compliance. The purpose of HR is to engage the only law firm asset: people. Client experience is predicated upon an exceptional employee experience. LP offers a competitive salary, attractive benefit package, and a comprehensive wellness program, but HR goes way beyond this basic starting point. Where HR really earns its stripes relative to the client experience is in navigating the working relationships of attorneys and legal coordinators (referred to as legal secretaries in many law firms). Engagement at this level is critical to identifying client experience opportunities.

Knowledge management

KM supports shared and efficient resources. In many respects, the LP Way is itself a shared resource. An effective KM approach is transparent, and propels collaboration. LP supports KM through an open contacts database, a robust intranet platform that houses shared form documents and research tools, and consistent content delivery channels for information at every level. LP embraces KM as a way of doing business and not as a separate function.

Records

This includes electronic and physical data, and often receives little attention in the client service delivery model. Think about how much time is spent in a law firm looking for the right file, document, version, and so on. The records area presents an excellent opportunity for high impact and immediate efficiency gains. Underinvesting in this area is a strategic misstep. LP increasingly relies less on paper. This is possible because every computer is equipped with a dual monitor, each administrative desk is equipped with a scanner, the document management and record management systems are integrated into a single platform, and LP has spent considerable time on user education in each of these areas. These factors encourage reliance predominately on electronic records over physical records, a behavior that easily transfers to increased client value.

Technology

Technology provides the tools that support the strategy, and not the other way around. Even a firm's basic technology budget can be an eye-popping figure, making it difficult to sell the need for investment beyond the basics of equipment, software, servers, storage, networks, backups, security, upgrades, helpdesk, and so on. However, technology offers many options to advance collaboration, decision making, and efficiency gains. The LP technology budget is presented in two categories: category one is the cost of doing business, much like rent or insurance, and requires little discussion and/or approval; category two is the fun part that proposes investments with solid business cases for adoption. There are many applications that propose to solve specific law firm challenges, but independent technology solutions are not always your friend. Significant resources can be spent just in trying to synchronize data flow. Coordination at a high level is imperative to making wise technology investment decisions. It is worth the effort to find or to create tools that enhance the firm goals. LP relies heavily on Microsoft SharePoint and Handshake Software to deliver information internally through a robust intranet and dashboard reporting system, and externally through a dedicated client extranet platform. The client extranet provides a direct client experience opportunity that has been extremely well received by clients.

Facilities

This is not the mail room. There is a huge opportunity to increase client and employee experience through facilities, beginning with the first impression created by reception to the layout and type of furniture selected for positive and collaborative working environments, to the type of food selected for productive meetings that support wellness. The facilities area is also instrumental in a firm's business continuity strategy, an area that is of great concern to clients. There are many studies about the positive impact on collaboration of sitting around a table sharing a meal. Think about a family setting where the kitchen is considered the heart of the home. In addition to the regular meetings over meal times where food is served, LP hosts weekly breakfasts and monthly lunches with no agenda. People sharing a meal and getting to know each other is powerful and leads to strong bonds and good working relationships. The dynamic of people who actually like working with each other is good for client experience.

Marketing

Marketing connects the dots and identifies opportunities for solidifying and growing client relationships. Marketing support at LP is connected to an overall business development approach that includes developing targeted prospective clients, as well as asking client intake questions designed to identify referral sources and client preferences in addition to the basic conflict information. LP business development professionals coach and accompany attorneys in client meetings and pitches and lead the client feedback program. There is no better way to enhance a client's experience than by asking them what they would like, and then actually delivering it.

Accounting

If there is a prize for the most overlooked opportunity for impacting a client experience, it goes to the accounting department and specifically to the billing function. A negative client experience at this level is usually indicative of a breakdown somewhere else along the way. Many missteps can be prevented with better and more frequent communication with the client and within the firm, among those working the file as well as among those managing the billing process. The primary goal in this area is to avoid surprises. In addition to this direct client contact, the accounting department houses most of the data that can be transformed into dashboards and other clever approaches to aid real-time decision making that contributes to a positive client experience.

Step 5: Ask for feedback

Self-awareness is paramount to the client experience. The final step of the LP Way is where the proverbial rubber meets the road. Anyone can produce a business strategy but to ask if it really works is not as easy. People are tricky and don't always share how they feel. Clients and employees will often just leave if they don't like something or if they had a bad experience. Further, it is often worse to ask and do nothing with the input than it is to not ask at all. Sometimes the feedback is hard to hear but it is truly a gift (even if it may feel as if wrapped in barbed wire). LP asks for feedback from all stakeholders in many ways.

Client interviews

Even before the LP Way was launched, LP incorporated client interviews into a client experience approach for many years. It is not complicated to ask clients how they feel, what they like and don't like, and yet, so many law firms still do not take this basic step. They assume that they already know or that they or their clients are too busy. Some of the best information is gathered from these discussions – insights that inform choices about resources, support, and strategic direction. Many client relationships have expanded based on this concept alone.

Partner surveys

"Do as I say, not as I do." This tongue-in-cheek quote may have originated in a law firm. The number one way for people to become disengaged is to believe there are different rules for leadership (or partnership) than there are for everyone else. The client experience bus does not even leave the station if engaged employees are not on board. The LP partner survey has gained much attention over the years but it works because it is the clearest accountability example of the firm's non-negotiable values (remember step 1?). Each person in the firm is asked to provide feedback about every partner. Survey responses are anonymous and the results are published internally. Partner surveys serve as an important compensation tool.

Operational effectiveness survey

People are invited to share ideas, suggestions, and even complaints about how the firm is performing in all of the areas encompassed by the LP Way. They are asked everything from the quality of communication from leadership, to the fairness of the compensation system, to the responsiveness of the help desk, and everything in between. Results from this survey are anonymous and also published internally.

Stay interviews

These are my favorite interviews. People are interviewed on the way in and on the way out of a firm, but rarely are those who are relied upon to support the most important clients, and to generally provide the most and steadfast value, asked about why they stay. This process requires trust in the interviewer and in the confidentiality of responses. When these conditions exist, the information gleaned is overwhelmingly well-considered and actionable, a virtual treasure chest.

In addition to these tools, the managing partner and executive director of the firm periodically host open meetings where attendees are encouraged to ask questions and to share their experiences. Hard questions indicate that people are paying attention and that they care. Firm leadership respects the "hot seat" as a pathway to deep insights that lead to a better experience.

The Waysayers

John Kotter is a world-renowned change management expert. In his book, *Leading Change*,[3] Kotter lists eight steps (another "step" strategy) necessary for a successful change program. The second step, form a guiding coalition, explains that a team with enough power and influence in the organization to lead the change effort must be assembled. Successful change cannot be championed by a single person alone, no matter how passionate or visionary. The LP Way guiding coalition is the LP Waysayers.

The LP Waysayers comprises "star contributors", identified by executive committee members during the initial roll-out meetings. The Waysayers continued in the direction of hosting mixed group meetings to discuss the LP Way. They took a deep dive into each step, soliciting participation and understanding of each person's contribution to the client experience. When exploring step 1, the Waysayers captured the discussions in a word cloud to depict the LP image and brand as seen through the eyes of LP employees (see Figure 2).

The LP Waysayers also hosted LP Think Tank, a take on the popular TV show, *Shark Tank*, in connection with step 4. Groups were challenged to focus on innovation in delivering legal services. Several groups presented their innovations to a panel of judges who were also LP clients. Talk about asking for feedback!

The Waysayers have become less active now that the LP Way is a way of life at LP, but their role was instrumental in getting everyone in the firm to rally around the client experience. They remain engaged and ready to champion the client experience at every opportunity.

Figure 2: The LP Way word cloud

Results

Providing the structure is the starting point. The magic happens when each individual embraces their role in the delivery cycle. Leadership communications at LP continually emphasize the connection of the LP Way to the client experience. The LP Way works because people understand not only what it is but why it exists. Simon Sinek, in his book *Start With Why*,[4] stresses the importance of leaders inspiring action by connecting them to "why". We have seen the amazing impact of this concept at LP.

The LP Way works when we see improved margins and realization rates in practices that embrace P3. The LP Way works when people at all levels hold each other accountable for LP's non-negotiable values. The LP Way works when the usually silent people speak up to share an idea. The LP Way works when clients go out of their way to thank us for creating such a positive experience.

LP believes that "what gets measured gets done". Selecting the "right" measurements is a strategic endeavor. LP measurements are continually revisited for the sake of the client experience. Building an unparalleled and consistent client experience is a journey that requires constant tending and adjustment. Agility is essential for successful execution of the LP Way strategy.

Conclusion

The LP Way is a strategy, not a slogan. A competitive advantage lies in the execution of this business plan. Many law firms highlight client service as a way to distinguish themselves from the competition but, when you look beneath the surface, there is often little connection to how the firm is structured, how it operates, and the type of culture it fosters. Everything is connected in a law firm.

Readers of a book by this title may wonder what all of this has to do with revenue growth. Here is the answer: *a positive client experience grows revenue.* Look no further for validation than Disney, the Ritz Carlton, Zappos or any other organization relentlessly focused on the client experience. It is simple to state but not so simple to do, particularly in a law firm environment full of autonomous people who earn a living by challenging the rules.

At the end of the day, law firms are defined by clients, and good lawyers are everywhere. These two truths force differentiation as a competitive strength. For LP, the difference is the intentional client experience.

During a recent interview, an LP client made this observation:

> *"LP is the poster child for awesome service and over-delivering. We are fortunate to have them as part of our team. In reality, it is not a client-law firm relationship. LP feels more like a business strategy partner."*

This is the LP Client Experience.

References

1. Collins, J., *Good to Great: Why Some Companies Make the Leap... and Others Don't*, London: Random House Business Books, 2001.
2. See www.lplegal.com for case studies of the journey and the impact of some of the process improvement projects.
3. Kotter, J. P., *Leading Change*, Massachusetts: Harvard Business Review Press, 1996.
4. Sinek, S. P., *Start With Why: How Great Leaders Inspire Everyone to Take Action*, Portfolio Penguin, 2009.